CHARTS OF
CHRISTIAN
THEOLOGY
AND
DOCTRINE

Books in the Zondervan*Charts* Series

CHARTS OF CHRISTIAN THEOLOGY AND DOCTRINE

H. WAYNE HOUSE

ZONDERVAN™

GRAND RAPIDS, MICHIGAN 49530

ZONDERVAN™

Charts of Christian Theology and Doctrine
Copyright © 1992 by H. Wayne House

Requests for information should be addressed to:

Zondervan, *Grand Rapids, Michigan 49530*

Library of Congress Cataloging-in-Publication Data

House, H. Wayne.
 Charts of Christian theology and doctrine/ by H. Wayne House.
  p. cm.
 ISBN 0-310-41661-2
 1. Theology — Doctrinal — Outline, syllabi, etc. I. Title.
BT77.3.H68 1992
230'.02'02—dc20   92-8489
                                                                CIP

Edited by Leonard G. Goss and Gerard Terpstra

Printed in the United States of America

01 02 03 04 05 06 /❖ CH/ 20 19 18 17 16 15

To
W. Robert Cook,
from whom I learned my basic theology,
and
Earl D. Radmacher,
teacher, friend, and my adopted spiritual father,
from whom I learned to live my theology

Contents

Preface

Putting together this book of charts on theology and doctrine has been a long but fruitful task. Ever since I began teaching theology at LeTourneau University and then at Dallas Theological Seminary, I felt that a basic charts book similar to my *Chronological and Background Charts to the New Testament* needed to be done. There is no attempt in this volume to provide an exhaustive analysis or overview of theology. Rather, my desire has been to state as fairly as I could different perspectives of various subjects within theology often of interest to or at least encountered by students of theology. Primarily I have followed a classical approach to theology, which may disappoint a few scholars, but I believe this will be more beneficial overall to teachers, students, and laypersons, who comprise those who will mainly use this work. Theology has fallen on bad times in some circles but to those who truly cherish the Word of God and desire to know what God is seeking to reveal to His people, it is a necessary and glorious task. I hope that all those who use this book will gain the kind of value that I have gained from writing it. It is inevitable that different kinds of mistakes occur in producing a book like this with its myriad of details. I will be happy to correct those for future editions as readers make me aware of them.

H. Wayne House
St. Patrick's Day, March 17, 1992

Soli Deo Gloria!

Acknowledgments

Many people were influential in the production of this book. I wish to thank the students of my various theology classes at Dallas Theological Seminary, especially the following who rendered special assistance to me in the production of these charts: Mark Allen, Rod Chaney, Kathie Church, Larry Gilcrease, Alan K. Ginn, Casey Jones, Mike Justice, Johann Lai, Randy Knowles, Toni Martin, Doreen Mellott, Steve Pogue, Greg Powell, Brian Rosner, David Seider, Brian Smith, Gayle Sumner, Larry Trotter. I give a special thanks to Richard Greene, Greg Trull, and Steve Rost, student research assistants and friends who labored with me on this project and others as a service of love to a fellow brother in Christ. If there are others, I beg forgiveness for my forgetfulness.

Also certain student assistants at Western Baptist College were helpful when I was dean and professor of theology at that school: Rob Baddeley, Marie Thompson, Toni Powell and Colleen Schneider Frazier. Also many thanks to Professor Tim Anderson.

Also I wish to express gratitude for my colleagues at Dallas Seminary (Craig Blaising, Lanier Burns, Norman Geisler, Fred Howe, Robert Lightner, and Ken Sarles) who looked over the different charts that related to their specialities in theology.

Gregg Harris was a great encouragement to me in deciding to undertake the production of this book using my Macintosh computer and Aldus PageMaker. Thank you Gregg.

Stan Gundry and Len Goss at Zondervan have been more than patient in waiting for the completion of this work. They have exhibited Christian grace and understanding to me over the last few years far beyond what could have been expected of them. I truly thank the Lord for them.

Finally, I wish to thank my wife, Leta, and children, Carrie and Nathan, who have been a blessing from God to me over the years. Their support has truly been one of God's wonderful gifts to me.

1. Distinctive Traits of Theological Systems

Traditional Roman Catholic Theology

Nature of Theology	Theology is constantly evolving in its understanding of the Christian faith. The Ignatian principle of accommodation and J. H. Newman's principle of development reflect the changing nature of Roman Catholic theology. Catholicism's trait of change is due mainly to the authoritative position given to church teaching.
Revelation	The Bible, including the Apocrypha, is recognized as the authoritative source of revelation as well as tradition and church teaching. The pope also makes authoritative pronouncements *ex cathedra* (from the chair) on issues of doctrine and morals; these pronouncements are immune from error. The church is the mother, guardian, and interpreter of the canon. Many post-Vatican II Roman Catholic scholars have deviated from the traditional teaching of the church in this area, have embraced higher critical perspectives on Scripture, and have rejected the infallibility of the pope.
Salvation	Saving grace is communicated through the seven sacraments, which are means of grace. Baptism, Confirmation, and Eucharist deal with initiation into the church. Penance and Anointing are concerned with healing. Marriage and Orders are sacraments of commitment and vocation. The Church administers the sacraments through the ordained hierarchically ordered priesthood. The traditional view was that there was no salvation outside the church but recent teaching has recognized grace may be received outside the church. In the sacrament of the Eucharist, the bread and the wine become the actual body and blood of Christ (transubstantiation).
Church	The four essential qualities of the true church are unity, holiness, catholicity, and apostolicity. Fundamentally the church is the ordained hierarchy, reaching its apex in the pope. Organization is built around a centralized priestly authority beginning with Peter. The authority of the priesthood is derived through apostolic succession in the church. Bishops in Rome have power to evaluate findings of schools and make pronouncements and conciliar definitions. The church is the mediator of Christ's presence in the world. God uses the church as his agent to move the world toward his kingdom.
Mary	At the Council of Ephesus (A.D. 431) Mary was declared to be the mother of God as well as the mother of Jesus Christ in the sense that the Son she bore was both God and man. Four Marian feasts (annunciation, purification, assumption, and nativity of Mary) are observed. Mary was without original sin or personal sin due to the intervention of God (immaculate conception). Mary is the merciful mediator between man and Christ the Judge.

3

Portions of this chart rely on material from *Tensions in Contemporary Theology*, eds. Stanley N. Gundry and Alan F. Johnson (Chicago: Moody Press, 1976.). Used by permission.

1. Distinctive Traits (continued)

Natural Theology

Definition	Natural theology is the attempt to attain an understanding of God and his relationship to the universe by means of rational reflection, without appealing to special revelation such as the self-revelation of God in Christ and in Scripture.
Epistemological Foundation	God is the eternal, unchanging, sovereign, holy, personal God, creator of the universe. He has everything in his control and through his eternal decrees from eternity has planned the future. It is done in such a way that he is not morally responsible for evil.
Relation to Revealed Theology	Natural theology deals with God's existence and attributes from sources common to all men (creation, logical reasoning, etc.) whereas revealed theology deals with specific truth discerned from the Scripture. Natural theology requires reason alone whereas revealed theology requires also faith and the illumination of the Spirit.
Purpose of Natural Theology	Natural theology can be used apologetically to prove the existence of God. It also supports revealed theology. If the conclusions of natural theology are accepted, then it would be "reasonable" also to accept revealed theological truth. Thus natural theology has an evangelistic purpose.
Possible Objections	Natural theology lacks a biblical basis. Natural theology attempts to exempt reason from the effects of the fall and of depravity.

Lutheran Theology

Theology	Theology builds around the three fundamental doctrines of *sola scriptura* (Scripture alone), *sola gratia* (grace alone), and *sola fide* (faith alone).
Christ	Christ is the center of Scripture. His person and work, especially his substitutionary death, are the basis of Christian faith and the message of salvation.
Revelation	Scripture alone is the authoritative source for theology and for church life and teaching. Scripture is the very Word of God and is as truthful and authoritative as God himself. At the center of Scripture stands the person and work of Christ. Thus Scripture's main purpose is soteriological--to proclaim the salvation message in Jesus Christ. The Word through Christ's work is God's mode of salvation.

1. Distinctive Traits (continued)

Salvation	Salvation comes only by grace through faith. The source of salvation is God's grace shown through Christ's work, the ground for salvation. The means for receiving salvation is faith only.
	People contribute nothing toward their salvation. They are totally without a free will in respect to salvation, and thus God is the efficient cause of salvation.
	The Spirit works through the word of the Gospel (including baptism and the Eucharist) to bring salvation.
	The Spirit uses the baptism of infants to produce faith in them and bring them to salvation.
	The Eucharist involves the actual presence of Christ with the bread and the wine though these elements remain bread and wine (consubstantiation).
	The theology of the cross is to be the mark of true theology. Instead of centering on the things about God's invisible nature and works as discussed in natural theology, which Luther calls a theology of glory, Christians are to focus on the humility of God revealed in the death of Christ on the cross. In a theology of the cross, the believers come to have a knowledge of God and also a true knowledge of themselves and their relationship to God.

Anabaptist Theology

Theology	Anabaptists did not stress systematic theological studies. Rather, doctrine was forged as it applied to life. Anabaptists were characterized by missionary zeal, separation of life, and an emphasis on ecclesiology.
Revelation	The Bible is to be obeyed completely in one's life. It is the sole authority and guide. The Spirit reveals the message of the Word to the believing community. Interpretation of Scripture is discerned primarily at church gatherings. Anabaptists tend to focus on the teachings of Christ and the New Testament more than on the Old Testament.
Salvation	Sin is not so much a bondage of the free will of man as it is a lost capacity to respond to God. The free will of man allows him to repent and be obedient to the gospel. When one repents and believes, God regenerates him to walk in new life. The emphasis is more on obedience than on sin, more on regeneration than on justification.
Church	The church is a visible body of believers obedient to Christ. The church exists as a visible fellowship, not an invisible body or a state church.
	Only believing adults can participate in baptism. Baptism testifies to the believer's separation from the world and commitment to obeying Christ.
	The sacraments–baptism and the Lord's Supper–are only symbols of Christ's work; they impart no grace to the participant. The characteristics of a church member's life ought to be personal conversion, a holy life, suffering for Christ, separation, love for the brethren, nonresistance, and obedience to the Great Commission. The church is a kingdom of God that is in constant conflict with the evil kingdom in the world system. The church is to evangelize in the world but not to participate in its system. This precludes participation in any governmental office or military service.

1. Distinctive Traits (continued)

	Reformed Theology
Theology	Reformed theology builds around the central theme of the sovereignty of God. The whole of reality falls under the supreme rule of God.
God	God is sovereign. He is perfect in every respect and holds all righteousness and power. He created all things and sustains them. As the Creator, he is in no way limited by creation.
Revelation	Reformed theology rests on Scripture alone (*sola scriptura*). The Bible is God's Word and as such remains without error in every aspect. Scripture guides all of church life and teaching. The Bible is authoritative in every area it addresses.
Salvation	God in eternity past chose a number of fallen creatures to be reconciled to himself. In time Christ came to save the chosen. The Holy Spirit enlightens the elect ones so that they can believe the Gospel and receive salvation. The elect can never resist the work of the Spirit nor fall away after receiving salvation. Salvation can be summarized by the Five Points of Calvinism: **T**otal Depravity, **U**nconditional Election, **L**imited Atonement, **I**rresistible Grace, and **P**erseverance of the Saints (TULIP).
Church	The church is composed of God's elect who have received salvation. They are bound by God's covenant to serve him in the world. Baptism symbolizes entry into the covenant body for both children and adults though either can renounce their baptism. When the believers partake in the Lord's Supper in faith, the Holy Spirit works in them to make them spiritual participants. Generally, elders, elected by the church, teach and oversee the local church body. The unity of the church must be grounded in doctrinal agreement.

1. Distinctive Traits (continued)

	Arminian Theology
Theology	Arminian theology is concerned to preserve the justice (fairness) of God. How could a just God hold individuals responsible for obedience to commands they are powerless to obey. Emphasizes divine foreknowledge, human responsibility and free will, and universal (common) enabling grace.
God	God is sovereign but has chosen to grant free will to human beings.
Salvation	God predestined to salvation those who he foreknew would repent and believe (conditional election). Christ suffered for the sins of all mankind, thus the atonement is unlimited. Salvation can be lost by a believer, and so one must strive not to fall and be lost. Christ did not pay the penalty for our sins, for if he had, then all would be saved. Rather, Christ suffered for our sins so the Father can forgive those who repent and believe. Christ's death was an example of the penalty of sin and the cost of forgiveness.

	Wesleyan Theology
Theology	Wesleyan theology is essentially Arminian but has a stronger sense of the reality of sin and of dependence on divine grace.
Revelation	The Bible is divine revelation, the ultimate standard for faith and practice. However, there are four means by which truth is mediated–Scripture, reason, tradition, and experience (the Wesleyan quadrilateral). Scripture has supreme authority. Next to Scripture, experience stands as the best evidence of Christianity.
Salvation	Salvation is a three-step process of grace: prevenient grace, justifying grace, and sanctifying grace. Prevenient grace is the universal work of the Spirit between one's birth and salvation. Prevenient grace prevents one from moving too far from God and enables one to respond, positively or negatively, to the gospel. To those who receive the gospel, justifying grace produces salvation and begins the process of sanctification. The believer has as a goal the achievement of entire sanctification, produced by the Holy Spirit in a second work of grace Entire sanctification means that one has been perfected in love. Perfection is not absolute but relative and dynamic. When one can love without self-interest or impure motive, then he or she has achieved perfection.

1. Distinctive Traits (continued)

	Liberal Theology
Theology	Liberal theologians seek to articulate Christianity in terms of contemporary culture and thinking. They attempt to maintain the essence of Christianity in modern terms and images.
God	God is immanent. He dwells within the world and is not above it or apart from it. Thus there stands no distinction between the natural and the supernatural.
Trinity	The Father works not supernaturally but through culture, philosophy, education, and society. Liberal theology is usually unitarian rather than Trinitarian, recognizing only the deity of the Father. Jesus was "full of God" but was not God incarnate. The Spirit is not a person within the Godhead but is simply God's activity in the world.
Christ	Christ gave a moral example for humanity. He also expressed God to us. Christ did not die to pay the penalty of our sins or impute his righteousness to man. He was neither God nor savior but merely God's representative.
Holy Spirit	The Spirit is the activity of God in the world, not a third person of the Godhead who is equal in essence to the Father and the Son.
Revelation	The Bible is a fallible human record of religious experiences and thought. The historical validity of the biblical record is doubted. Scientific assessments prove the miraculous in the Bible to be religious expression only.
Salvation	Man is not innately sinful but possesses a universal religious sentiment. The goal of salvation is not personal conversion but societal improvement. Christ set the ultimate example of what mankind is striving for and will ultimately become. Liberal theology has characteristically uniformly denied the Fall, original sin, and the substitutionary nature of the Atonement.
Future	Christ will not personally return. The kingdom will come to earth as a result of a universal moral development.

1. Distinctive Traits (continued)

Existential Theology

Theology	Existential theologians claim that we have to "demythologize" Scripture. "To demythologize Scripture is to reject not Scripture or the Christian message, but the world-view of a past epoch." That means to explain everything supernatural as myth. The important part of Christian faith consequently becomes a subjective experience, rather than an objective truth (see Salvation). The Bible, when demythologized, does not talk about God, but about man.
God	Objective knowledge of God's existence is not possible. The concept of God was a help for the early Christians to understand themselves, but in our time, with a different world-view, we can see behind the myth. Thus, God is our statement about human life. "It is therefore clear that if a man will speak about God, he must evidently speak of himself" (Bultmann). If God exists, he works in the world as if he does not exist. And we cannot know about him in any objective way.
Trinity	The Trinity is a myth relating to the supernatural content of the Bible (see God).
Christ	Jesus is just a common man. As the New Testament is called myth, we do not have much, if any, knowledge of the "historical Jesus." That leaves us a picture of Jesus without any "divine" intervention. The Cross has no significance regarding the vicarious bearing of sins, and the Resurrection is utterly inconceivable as an historical event. This is also true of the Virgin Birth and other miracles.
Holy Spirit	All we know about the Holy Spirit belongs to the untrustworthy supernatural parts of the Bible, which are really only mythical.
Revelation	The Bible is not a source of objective information about God. To understand themselves better people in the first centuries created a myth around Jesus. He did not perform miracles nor rise from the dead. If we can "strip the myths" from the Gospel, we discover the original purpose behind the myth and can find guidance for our lives today. This is called "demythologization." The Bible becomes a book that has as its aim to transform persons through encounter.
Salvation	"Salvation" is to find one's "true self." This is done by a choice to put our faith in God, and this choice will change our view of ourselves. Salvation, then, is a change of our whole outlook and conduct in life, built on an experience of "God"; it is not a change of man's nature. As we do not know anything about God objectively, it is a matter of "faith in faith."
Myth	Bultmann understood myth as a way to speak of the Transcendent in terms of this world: "Mythology is that form of imagery in which that which is not of this world, that which is divine, is represented as though it were of this world and human; 'the beyond' is represented as 'the here and now.'"

1. Distinctive Traits (continued)

Neo-orthodox Theology

Theology	Neo-orthodoxy is more a hermeneutic than it is a complete systematic theology. It reacted against late-nineteenth-century liberalism and strove to retain the essence of Reformation theology while still adapting to contemporary issues. It is a theology of encounter between God and man.
God	God is wholly transcendent except when he chooses to reveal himself to man. God is totally sovereign over and free from his creation. God cannot be known through proofs (Kierkegaard). God cannot be known through objective doctrine but through an experience of revelation.
Christ	Christ as manifested in Scripture is the Christ of faith, not necessarily the historical Jesus. Christ is the revelation of God. The important Christ is the one experienced by the individual. Christ was not virgin-born (Brunner). Christ is the symbol of the new being in which all that estranges people from God is dissolved (Tillich).
Revelation	God's revelation to man through his Word is threefold. Jesus is the Word made flesh. Scripture points to the Word. Preaching proclaims the Word made flesh. The Bible contains the Word of God. The Word is revealed by the Spirit as the Bible and Christ are proclaimed. The Bible is human and fallible and is reliable only to the extent that God reveals himself through encounters with Scripture. Historicity of Scripture is unimportant. Creation account is a myth (Niebuhr) or a saga (Barth).
Salvation	Man is completely sinful and can be saved only by God's grace. The Word produces a crisis decision between the rebellion of sin and the grace of God. Only by faith can a person choose God's grace in this crisis and receive salvation. All mankind is elect in Christ (Barth). There is no such thing as inherited sin from Adam (Brunner). Man sins by choice, not because of nature (Brunner). Sin is self-centeredness (Brunner). Sin is social injustice and fear (Niebuhr). Salvation is commitment to God in a blind "leap of faith" while in despair (Kierkegaard).
Eschatology	Eternal punishment and hell are not realities (Brunner).

1. Distinctive Traits (continued)

Liberation Theology

Theology	Theology is not seen as a system of dogmas but rather as a way to initiate social change. This view has been called the "liberation of theology" (H. Segundo). This theology grew out of Vatican II and the liberal theologians' attempts to wrestle with social, political, and economic inequities in the face of a Christianity no longer based on a biblical world view. Much of the setting for liberation theology has been Latin America, and this theology has become an answer to the political oppression of the poor. The proponents often have different views; there is really no "unified" liberation theology. Rather, it is a number of closely related "alternatives" springing from common roots. Rather than a classical theology concerned with such theological matters as the nature of God, man, or the future, liberation theology is concerned with this world and how changes may occur through political action. In Latin America, especially, Roman Catholic theologians have sought to combine Christianity and Marxism.
God	God is active, always taking sides with the poor and oppressed and against the oppressors, so that he does not work equally for all. Liberation theologians emphasize immanence to the neglect of transcendence. He is mutable.
Christ	Jesus is seen as a messiah of political involvement. He is God entering the struggle for justice on the side of the poor and the oppressed. However, he was not a savior in the traditional meaning of the word. Instead, liberation theologians support a "moral influence" view of the atonement. There is no thought of a satisfaction of God's wrath against man.
Holy Spirit	Pneumatology is virtually absent in liberation theology. It seems hard to find a role for the work of the Holy Spirit in the man-centered political systems.
Revelation	The Bible is not a book of eternal truths and rules, but a book of specific (but often unreliable accounts of) history. However, many texts are used in support of this theology, especially the account of the Exodus. Liberation theologians use the "new" hermeneutics in order to defend their view. Because their theology is built on a Marxist analysis and seen as a useful way of creating "proper" actions (see Salvation), they primarily emphasize ethics that achieve the ends of the movement.
Salvation	Salvation is viewed as social change in society where justice for the poor and oppressed is established. "The Catholic who is not a revolutionary is living in mortal sin" (C. Torres). Any method to that end is acceptable, even violence and revolution. The view tends toward universalism, and evangelism becomes merely an effort to create awareness to prepare people for political action.
Church	The church is perceived as a means to change society: "The pastoral activity of the church does not flow as a conclusion from theological premises . . . [it] tries to be part of the process through which the world is transformed" (G. Gutiérrez). Political neutrality is not an option for the church.

1. Distinctive Traits (continued)

Black Theology

Theology	Black theology is a form of liberation theology that has its center in the theme of oppression of blacks by whites. It came out of the "need for black people to define the scope and meaning of black existence in a white racist society" (Cone). It emerged in the last two decades in the wave of liberation movements as an expression of black consciousness and seems to speak to the issues that blacks must contend with on a daily basis.
God	Intricate and largely philosophical views of God are largely ignored in preference for concerns of the oppressed. White Christian concepts taught to the black man thus are to be disregarded or ignored. God's person, the Trinity, his supreme power and authority as well as "subtle indications of God's white maleness" are said not to relate to (and in some cases are antagonistic to) the black experience. The dominant perspective on God is God in action, delivering the oppressed because of his righteousness. His immanence is stressed over his transcendence, and as a result he is seen to be in flux or always changing.
Trinity	The Trinity is not stressed. However, Jesus is God, but in the sense of God's visible expression of concern and salvation.
Christ	He is One who delivers, almost exclusively, in social ways. He is a liberator, or "Black Messiah" whose work of emancipation for the poor and rejected of society is the parallel to the blacks' quest for liberation. Christ's message is "black power" (Henry). His intrinsic nature and spiritual activity receive little or no attention. Some even deny his role as the atoning sacrifice for the world's sins and provider of eternal life (Shrine).
Revelation	Black theology is not bound to biblical literalism but is of a more pragmatic nature. Only the experience of black oppression is the authoritative standard.
Salvation	Salvation is freedom from oppression and pertains to blacks in this life. Proponents of black theology are concerned specifically with the political and theological aspects of salvation more than the spiritual. In other words, salvation is physical liberation from white oppression rather than freedom from the sinful nature and acts of each individual person. Presenting heaven as a reward for following Christ is seen as an attempt to dissuade blacks from the goal of real liberation of their whole persons.
Church	The church is the focus of social expression in the black community where the blacks can express freedom and equality (Cone). Thus the church and politics have formed a cohesion where the theological expression of the desire for social freedom is carried out.

2. Contemporary Feminist Theological Models

Roots of Feminist Theology

The rise of the Women's Liberation Movement from the mid-20th century helped to create a feminist critical consciousness. That consciousness, interacting with the Bible and Christian theological traditions has called for a new investigation of past paradigms and a new agenda for study. This "new" investigation and agenda have resulted in the following models.

Model	Proponents	Viewpoint
Rejectionist (Post-Christian)		Sees the Bible as promoting an oppressive patriarchal structure and rejects it as nonauthoritative.
Rejection Wing	B. Friedan, K. Millett, G. Steinem	Rejects whole Judeo-Christian traditions as hopelessly male-oriented.
Restoration Wing	M. Daly, N. Goldenberg	Restores the religion of witchcraft or accepts a nature mysticism based exclusively on women's consciousness.
Loyalist (Evangelical)		Sees no radically oppressive sexism in the biblical record.
Traditional Wing	J. Hurley, S. Foh, S. Clark, G. Knight, E. Elliot, Council on Biblical Manhood and Woman-hood	Seeks order through complementary roles. The role of women in God's created order is to be fulfilled through voluntary submission and dependence in church and family (and some in society). The divine pattern for men is loving leadership. This will not diminish the true freedom and dignity of women.
Egalitarian Wing	C. Kroeger, A. Spencer, G. Bilizikian, Christians for Biblical Equality	The Bible calls for mutual submission with neither male nor female relegated to any particular role in home, church, or society based solely on gender.
Reformist (Liberation)		With rejectionists sees patriarchal chauvinism in the Bible and Christian history and has a desire to overcome it. Its commitment to liberation as the central message of the Bible keeps it from discarding the Christian tradition.
Moderate Wing	L. Scanzoni, V. Mollenkott, M. S. van Leeuwen	Through exegesis tries to bring to light the positive role of women in the Bible. Some moderate reformists search for a "usable" hermeneutic or liberation in the prophetic tradition. In texts not dealing specifically with women, they find a call to create a just society free from any kind of social, economic, or sexist oppression.
Radical Wing	E. Schüssler, E. Stanton	Calls for a more far-reaching feminist "hermeneutic of suspicion." It begins with the acknowledgment that the Bible has been written, translated, canonized, and interpreted by males. The canon of faith has become male-centered. Women, through theological and exegetical reconstruction, must enter again the center stage they occupied in early Christian history.

13

3. Guide to Interpretation of Biblical Texts

	Descriptive What does it mean?	Rational Why was this said here?	Implicational What is the significance?
Terms	What is meant by the term? How does it function in this sentence? What key words need word study?	Why is this term used? (generally) Why is this term used? (specifically) Why is this a key term in the passage?	What are the dominant truths taught in the passage? What do these truths imply about how God acts or wants believers to act?
Structure	What kind of sentence is it? What laws of structure are used? contrast cause/effect comparison summation/explanation repetition question/answer proportion general/specific climax interchange/inversion What are the major connector words?	Why was this style of sentence used? What are the causes, effects, or purposes reflected in the clauses? Why is this order of words, phrases, or clauses used? Why are the stated relationships as they are?	What are the abiding truths taught in the main statements? What major motivations or promises do the subordinate clauses reveal? What major ideas are emphasized by the order of the words or phrases? What limitations are found?
Literary Form	What literary form is used? What are its characteristics? How does this literary form convey the meaning of the author? Is the language literal or figurative?	Why is this literary form employed? Why are the figures used as they are?	What is the significance of this form of literature as related to the truth conveyed? What light is shed on the truth by the figures of speech used?
Atmosphere	What aspects of the passage reveal the atmosphere? What emotional words are used? How is the author's attitude developed in the text? the readers'?	Why does this kind of atmosphere dominate this particular passage? Why is this atmosphere essential to the effective presentation of this passage?	What is the significance of atmosphere to the argument of the passage? Is encouragement or rebuke the major tenor of the passage?

4. A Comparison of Covenant Theology and Dispensationalism

Viewpoint	Covenant Theology	Dispensationalism
Description	Covenant theology centers on one overall major covenant known as the covenant of grace. Some have called it the covenant of redemption. By many this is defined as an eternal covenant among the members of the Godhead including the following elements: (1) the Father chose a people to be his own; (2) the Son was designated with his agreement to pay the penalty of their sin; and (3) the Holy Spirit was designated with his agreement to apply the work of the Son to this chosen people." This covenant of grace is being worked out on earth in history through subordinate covenants, beginning with the covenant of works and culminating in the new covenant, which fulfills and completes God's work of grace to man on earth. These covenants include the Adamic covenant, Noahic covenant, Abrahamic covenant, Mosaic covenant, Davidic covenant, and new covenant. The covenant of grace is also used to explain the unity of redemption through all ages beginning with the Fall when the covenant of works ended. Covenant theology does not see each covenant as separate and distinct. Instead, each covenant builds on the previous ones, including aspects of previous covenants and culminating in the new covenant.	Dispensational theology looks on the world and the history of mankind as a household over which God is superintending the outworking of his purpose and will. This outworking of his purpose and will can be seen by noting the various periods or stages of different economies whereby God deals with his work and mankind in particular. These various stages or economies are called dispensations. Their number may include as many as seven: innocence, conscience, human government, promise, law, grace, and kingdom.
God's People	God has one people, represented by the saints of the Old Testament era and the saints of the New Testament era.	God has two people–Israel and the church. Israel is an earthly people, and the church his heavenly people.
God's Plan for His People	God has one people, the church, for whom he has one plan in all the ages since Adam: to call out this people into one body in both the Old and New Testament ages.	God has two separate peoples, Israel and the church, and also has two separate plans for these two distinct peoples. He plans an earthly kingdom for Israel. This kingdom has been postponed until Christ's coming in power, since Israel rejected it at Christ's first coming. During the church age God is calling out a heavenly people. Dispensationalists disagree over whether the two peoples will remain distinct in the eternal state.
God's Plan of Salvation	God has one plan of salvation for his people since the time of Adam. The plan is one of grace, being an outworking of the eternal covenant of grace and comes through faith in Jesus Christ.	God has only one plan of salvation, though this has often been misunderstood because of inexactness in some dispensational writings. Some have wrongly taught or understood that Old Testament believers were saved by works and sacrifices. However, most have believed that salvation has always been by grace through faith, but that the content of the faith may vary until the full revelation of God in Christ.

15

This chart represents traditional views and is based chiefly on the study of Richard P. Belcher, *A Comparison of Dispensationalism and Covenant Theology* (Columbia, S.C.: Richbarry Press, 1986).

4. Covenant Theology/Dispensationalism (continued)

Viewpoint	Covenant Theology	Dispensationalism
The Place of Eternal Destiny for God's People	God has but one place for his people, since he has but one people, one plan, and one plan of salvation. his people will be in his presence for eternity.	There is disagreement among dispensationalists regarding the future state of Israel and the church. Many believe that the church will sit with Christ on his throne in the New Jerusalem during the millennium as he rules over the nations, while Israel will be the head of the nations on earth.
The Birth of the Church	The church existed prior to the New Testament era, including all the redeemed since Adam. Pentecost was not the beginning of the church but the empowering of the New Testament manifestation of God's people.	The church was born on the day of Pentecost and did not exist in history until that time. The church, the body of Christ, is not found in the Old Testament, and the Old Testament saints are not part of the body of Christ.
The Purpose of Christ's First Coming	Christ came to die for our sins and to establish the New Israel, the New Testament manifestation of the church. This continuation of God's plan placed the church under a new and better covenant, which was a new manifestation of the same Covenant of Grace. The kingdom that Jesus offered was the present, spiritual, and invisible kingdom. Some covenantalists (especially postmillennialists) also see a physical aspect to the kingdom.	Christ came to establish the messianic kingdom. Some dispensationalists believe that this was to be an earthly kingdom in fulfillment of the Old Testament promises to Israel. If the Jews had accepted Jesus' offer, this earthly kingdom would have been immediately established. Other dispensationalists believe that Christ did establish the messianic kingdom in some form in which the church participates but that the earthly kingdom awaits the second coming of Christ to the earth. Christ always intended the cross before the crown.
The Fulfillment of the New Covenant	The promises of the New Covenant mentioned in Jeremiah 31:31ff. are fulfilled in the New Testament.	Dispensationalists differ over whether only Israel is to participate in the New Covenant, at a later time, or whether both the church and Israel jointly participate. Some dispensationalists believe there is one new covenant with two applications: one for Israel and one for the church. Others believe that there are two new covenants: one for Israel and another one for the church.
The Problem of Amillennialism and Post-millennialism versus Pre-millennialism	Covenant theology has been amillennial historically, believing the kingdom to be present and spiritual, or postmillennial, believing the kingdom is being established on the earth with Christ's coming as the culmination. In recent years some covenant theologians have been premillennial, believing that there will be a future manifestation of God's kingdom on earth. However, God's dealings with Israel will be in connection with the church. Postmillennialists believe that the church is bringing in the kingdom now, with Israel ultimately to be made a part of the church.	All dispensationalists are premillennialists, though not necessarily pretribulationalists. Premillennialists of this type believe that God will turn to the nation of Israel again apart from his work with the church and that there will be a thousand–year period of Christ's reign on David's throne in accordance with and in fulfillment of the prophecies of the Old Testament.
The Second Coming of Christ	Christ's coming will be to bring final judgment and the eternal state. Those who are premillennial assert that a millennial period will precede the judg-ment and eternal state. Postmillen-nialists believe that the kingdom is being established by the work of God's people on the earth until the time when Christ will bring it to completion at his coming.	The Rapture will occur first, according to most, then a tribulation period, followed by a thousand–year reign of Christ, after which there will be judgment and the eternal state.

5. Representative Dispensational Schemes

J. N. Darby 1800-1882	J. H. Brookes 1830-1897	James M. Gray 1851-1935	C. I. Scofield 1843-1921
Paradisaical state (to the Flood)	Eden	Edenic	Innocency
	Anteadiluvian	Antediluvian	Conscience
Noah		Patriarchal	Human government
Abraham	Patriarchal		Promise
Israel-- under law under priesthood under kings	Mosaic	Mosaic	Law
Gentiles	Messianic	Church	Grace
Spirit	Holy Ghost		
Millennium	Millennial	Millennial	Kingdom
		Fullness of times	
		Eternal	

Adapted from Charles C. Ryrie, *Dispensationalism Today* (Chicago: Moody Press, 1965), p. 84. Used by permission.

6. Models of Revelation

Model	Adherents	Definition of Revelation	Purpose of Revelation
Revelation as Doctrine*	Patristic fathers Medieval church Reformers B. B. Warfield Francis Schaeffer International Council on Biblical Inerrancy	Revelation is divinely authoritative and is conveyed objectively and propositionally through the exclusive medium (words) of the Bible.** Its propositions generally assume the character of doctrine.	To elicit saving faith through acceptance of the truth as revealed ultimately in Jesus Christ.
Revelation as Historical	William Temple G. Ernest Wright Oscar Cullman Wolfhart Pannenberg	Revelation is the demonstration of God's saving disposition and capacity as witnessed by his great deeds in human history.	To instill hope and trust in the God of history.
Revelation as Inner Experience	Friedrich Schleiermacher D. W. R. Inge C. H. Dodd Karl Rahner	Revelation is the self-disclosure of God by his intimate presence in the depths of the human spirit and psyche.	To impart an experience of union with God that equates with immortality.
Revelation as Dialectical Presence	Karl Barth Emil Brunner John Baillie	Revelation is God's message to those whom he encounters with his Word in the Bible *and* with Christ in Christian proclamation.	To generate faith as the appropriate meta-revelatory completion of itself.
Revelation as New Awareness	Teilhard de Chardin M. Blondel Gregory Baum Leslie Dewart Ray L. Hart Paul Tillich	Revelation is one's arrival at a higher level of consciousness as one is attracted to a more fruitful sharing in the divine creativity.	To achieve the restructuring of perception/experience and a concomitant self-transformation.

*The doctrine model acknowledges "natural revelation" (that which may be discerned of God through reason or observing creation) apart from special biblical revelation. It is regarded to be of minor importance, however, since it is not salvific (it merely "pricks" the conscience). This model considers miracles and apostolic signs confirmations of revelation.
**Roman Catholic theologians adhering to this model add to this definition the words "or by official Church teaching."
This chart is based on Avery Dulles, *Models of Revelation* (Maryknoll, N.Y.: Orbis Books, 1992). Used by permission.

6. Models of Revelation (continued)

Model	General View of the Bible	Relation to History	Means of Human Apprehension
Revelation as Doctrine	The Bible *is* the Word of God (both in form and content).	Revelation is *trans-historical* (it is discrete and determinative with regard to its contiguity with history).	Illumination (by the Holy Spirit)
Revelation as Historical	The Bible is an *event*. It is conjunctive with God's self-revelation as disclosed indirectly through the totality of his activity in history. It is never extrinsic to either the continuity or particularity of that history.	Revelation is *intra-historical* (the Bible reveals history *within* history).	Reason
Revelation as Inner Experience	The Bible *contains* the word of God (inter-mingled with the human elements of error and myth: the Bible is a "husk" wrapped around the "kernel" of truth). That truth can be apprehended (experienced) only by personal illumination.	Revelation is *psycho-historical* (it relates to history as a mental image of human continuity).	Intuition
Revelation as Dialectical Presence	The Bible *becomes* the word of God to us (revelation is not static but dynamic and has to do with the contingency of human response) as it is empowered by the Holy Spirit.	Revelation is *supra-historical* (the Bible reveals "history *beyond* history").	"Transactional" reason (interaction with faith intrinsic to revelation)
Revelation as New Aware-ness	The Bible is a paradigm—a mediator through which self-transformation and transcen-dance may be achieved (but the Bible is only a human effort using "limping" human language pursuant to this end).	Revelation is *ahistorical* (history is rendered practically irrelevant as it is subjected to ongoing reinterpretations of personal transcendence).	Rational/mystical meditation

6. Models of Revelation (continued)

Model	Basic Hermeneutic	Purported Strengths	Purported Weaknesses
Revelation as Doctrine	Induction (objective)	It derives from the Bible's own testimony to itself. It is the traditional view from the patristic fathers to the present. It is distinctive by virtue of its internal coherence. It provides the basis for consistent theology.	The Bible does not claim propositional infallibility of itself. Early and medieval exegetes were amenable to allegorical/spiritual interpretations. The variety of literary terms and conventions argues against this model. Modern science refutes biblical literalism and other notions attached to this model. Its hermeneutic ignores the suggestive power of biblical context.
Revelation as Historical	Deduction (objective/subjective)	It has pragmatic religious value because of its concreteness. It identifies certain biblical themes minimized or ignored by the propositional model (Revelation as Doctrine). It is more organic in its approach and points to a pattern of history. It is nonauthoritarian and is thus more plausible to the contemporary mentality.	It relegates the Bible to a "phenomenon" status. It is virtually destitute of theological undergirding. Notwithstanding its alleged plausibility, it does not foster ecumenical dialogue.
Revelation as Inner Experience	Eclecticism (subjective)	It offers a defense against a rationalistic critique of the Bible. It promotes devotional life. Its flexibility encourages inter-religious dialogue.	It "picks and chooses" from the Bible. It substitutes natural elitism for the Biblical concept of election. It divorces revelation from doctrine by its emphasis on experience. Its experiential orientation also risks excessive introspection on the part of the devotionalist.
Revelation as Dialectical Presence	Induction (subjective)	It seeks to base itself on a biblical foundation. It evidences a clear, but not orthodox, Christological focus. Its emphasis on paradox removes many objections as to the implausibility of the Christian message. It offers the possibility of encounter with a transcendent God.	Though biblically based, it lacks internal coherence. Its paradoxical language is confusing. Its abstruseness with regard to relating the Christ of faith to the historical Jesus undermines its validity.
Revelation as New Awareness	Ultra-eclecticism (extremely subjective)	It escapes inflexibility and authoritarianism. It respects the active role of the person in the revelatory process. It harmonizes with evolutionist or transformationist thinking. Its philosophy satisfies the need of worldly fruitfulness.	It does violence to Scripture through its unorthodox interpretations. It is a neo-gnosticism that is inadequate to meaningful Christian experience. In its totality, it denies the cognitive/objective value of the Bible.

7. Views of General Revelation

Definition	General revelation is God's communication of himself to all persons at all times and in all places. It refers to God's self-manifestation through nature, history, and the inner being (consciousness) of the human person.
Thomas Aquinas	Aquinas is an advocate of natural theology, which says a true knowledge of God can be gained from the spheres of nature, history, and human personality apart from the Bible.
	All truth belongs to two realms. The lower realm is the realm of nature and is known by reason; the higher is the realm of grace and is accepted on authority by faith. Aquinas contended he could show by reason the existence of God and the immortality of the soul.
Roman Catholic Theology	General revelation provides a basis for the construction of natural theology. Roman Catholic theology is two-storied:
	Level One: Natural theology is built from building blocks of general revelation cemented into place by reason. This includes proofs for the existence of God and the immortality of the soul. It is insufficient for saving knowledge of God. Most do not arrive at this first level through reason but by faith.
	Level Two: A revealed theology is built from building blocks of special revelation cemented into place by faith. This includes substitutionary atonement, the Trinity, etc. On this level a person is brought to salvation.
John Calvin	God has given an objective, valid, rational revelation of himself in nature, history, and human personality. It can be observed by anyone. Calvin draws this conclusion from Psalm 19:1-2 and Romans 1:19-20. Sin has marred the witness of general revelation, and the testimony of God is blurred. General revelation does not enable the unbeliever to come to a true knowledge of God. What is needed is the spectacles of faith. When one is exposed to and regenerated through special revelation, he is enabled to see clearly what is in general revelation. But what one sees has always been genuinely and objectively there.
	One could find a natural theology in Romans 1:20, but Paul goes on to show that fallen man engages in suppression and substitution of the truth. Even the mention of nature in Psalm 19 was by a godly man who viewed nature through the perspective of special revelation.
Karl Barth	Barth rejects natural theology and general revelation. Revelation is redemptive in nature. To know God and to have current information about him is to be related to him in salvific experience.
	Human beings are not able to know God apart from revelation in Christ. If man could achieve some knowledge of God outside of his revelation in Jesus Christ, man would have contributed in some small measure to his salvation. Apart from the Incarnation there is no revelation. Romans 1:18-32 indicates that people do find God in the cosmos but only because they already know him from special revelation communicated by the Holy Spirit when one reads the Word of God.
	The Bible is only a record of revelation, an authoritative pointer to revelation.
Scripture Passages	Psalm 19 can be interpreted to mean that there is no language and no words whose voice is unheard. Verses 7-14 show how the law goes beyond revelation in the cosmos.
	Romans 1:18-32 emphasizes the revelation of God in nature. Romans 2:14-16 emphasizes general revelation in human personality. Paul makes the point in 1:18 that people have the truth but suppress it because of their unrighteousness. The wicked are without excuse because God has shown through creation what can be known about him. Romans 2 points out that the Jew fails to do what the law requires and the Gentile also knows enough to make him responsible to God.
	Acts 14:15-17 points out that people should turn to the living God, who made heaven and earth. Even though God permitted nations to go their own way, he left a witness in history and nature.
	Acts 17:22-31 records Paul's proclamation of the unknown God of the Athenians as the same God he knew from special revelation. They had sensed this unknown God with no special revelation. Verse 28 allows that even a pagan poet, without special revelation, had come to spiritual truth, though not to salvation.

8. The Modes of Special Revelation

MIRACULOUS EVENTS: God at work in concrete historical ways within the world, affecting what occurs

Examples:

    Call of Abram (Gen. 12)

    Birth of Isaac (Gen. 21)

    Passover (Exod. 12)

    Crossing of the Red Sea (Exod. 14)

DIVINE SPEECH: God's revelation through human language

Examples:

    Audible speech (God speaking to Adam in the garden,
        Gen. 2:16, and to Samuel in the temple,1 Sam. 3:4)

    The prophetic office (Deut. 18:15-18)

    Dreams (Daniel, Joseph)

    Visions (Ezekiel, Zechariah, John in Revelation)

    Scripture (2 Tim 3:16)

VISIBLE MANIFESTATIONS: God manifesting himself in visible form

Examples:

    Old Testament theophanies before the incarnation of Jesus
        Christ (usually described as the angel of Yahweh, Gen.
        16:7-14, or as a man as with Jacob, Gen. 32)

    Shekinah glory (Exod. 3:2-4; 24:15-18; 40:34-35)

    Jesus Christ (the unique manifestation of God as an actual
        human, with all the human processes and experiences such
        as birth, pain, and death, John 1:14; 14:9; Heb. 1:1-2)

9. Theories of Inspiration

Theories of Inspiration	Statement of the Viewpoints	Objections to the Viewpoint
Mechanical or Dictation	The biblical author is a passive instrument in the transmission of the revelation of God. The personality of the author is set aside to preserve the text from fallible human aspects.	If God had dictated the Scripture, the style, vocabulary, and writing would be uniform. But the Bible indicates diverse personalities and manners of expression in its writers.
Partial	Inspiration concerns only the doctrines of Scripture that were unknowable to the human authors. God provided the general ideas and trends of revelation but gave the human author freedom in the manner of expressing it.	It is not possible to inspire general ideas infallibly and yet not inspire the words of Scripture. The manner of giving words of revelation to the prophets and the degree of conformity to the very words of Scripture by Jesus and the apostolic writers indicate inspiration of all the biblical text, even the words.
Degrees of Inspiration	Certain portions of the Bible are more inspired or differently inspired than other portions. This views allows for errors of various sorts in the Scripture.	No suggestion of degrees of inspiration is found in the text (2 Tim. 3:16). The entire Scripture is incorruptible and cannot err (John 10:35; 1 Peter 1:23).
Intuition or Natural	Gifted individuals with exceptional insight were chosen by God to write the Bible. Inspiration is like an artistic ability or a natural endowment.	This view makes the Bible really no different from other inspirational religious or philosophical literature. The biblical text represents the Scripture coming from God through men (2 Peter 1:20-21).
Illumination or Mystical	The human authors were enabled by God to write the Scriptures. The Holy Spirit heightened their normal powers.	The biblical teaching indicatestion came through special divine communication, not through hieghtened capacities of men. The human authors express the very words of God, not merely their own words.
Verbal, Plenary	Both divine and human elements are present in the production of Scripture. The entire text of Scripture, including the very words, are a product of the mind of God expressed in human terms and conditions.	If every word of Scripture were a word of God, then there would not be the human element in the Bible that is observed.

10. Evangelical Theories on Inerrancy

Position	Proponent	Statement of Viewpoint
Complete Inerrancy	Harold Lindsell Roger Nicole Millard Erickson	The Bible is fully true in all it teaches or affirms. This extends to the areas of both history and science. It does not hold that the Bible has a primary purpose to present exact information concerning history and science. Therefore the use of popular expressions, approximations, and phenomenal language is acknowledged and is believed to fulfill the requirement of truthfulness. Apparent discrepancies, therefore, can and must be harmonized.
Limited Inerrancy	Daniel Fuller Stephen Davis William LaSor	The Bible is inerrant only in its salvific doctrinal teachings. The Bible was not intended to teach science or history, nor did God reveal matters of history or science to the writers. In these areas the Bible reflects the understanding of its culture and may therefore contain errors.
Inerrancy of Purpose	Jack Rogers James Orr	The Bible is without error in accomplishing its primary purpose of bringing people into personal fellowship with Christ. The Scriptures, therefore, are truthful (inerrant) only in that they accomplish their primary purpose, not by being factual or accurate in what they assert. (This view is similar to the Irrelevancy of Inerrancy view.)
The Irrelevancy of Inerrancy	David Hubbard	Inerrancy is essentially irrelevant for a variety of reasons: (1) Inerrancy is a negative concept. Our view of Scripture should be positive. (2) Inerrancy is an unbiblical concept. (3) Error in the Scriptures is a spiritual or moral matter, not an intellectual one. (4) Inerrancy focuses our attention on minutiae, rather than on the primary concerns of Scripture. (5) Inerrancy hinders honest evaluation of the Scriptures. (6) Inerrancy creates disunity in the church. (This view is similar to the Inerrancy of Purpose view.)

11. Approaches to Reconciling Discrepancies in Scripture

← M O R E   D E D U C T I V E ——

Strategy/Advocate	Explanation
The Abstract Approach B. B. Warfield	Those who follow this approach are aware that there are difficulties in Scripture, but they tend to feel that these difficulties do not all have to be explained because the weight of evidence for the inspiration and consequent inerrancy of the Bible is so great that no amount of difficulty could overthrow it. They tend to rest their case primarily on the doctrinal consideration of the Bible's inspiration.
The Harmonistic Approach Edward J. Young Louis Gaussen	Adherents of this approach hold that belief in inerrancy is based on the doctrinal teaching of inspiration. They assert that the difficulties presented can be resolved, and they attempt to do so—sometimes by the use of conjecture.
The Moderate Harmonistic Approach Everett Harrison	This approach follows the style of the harmonistic approach to a certain extent. The problems are taken seriously, and an effort is made to solve them or relieve the difficulties as far as this is reasonably possible with the data currently available. Attempts are not made prematurely.
The Errant Source Approach* Edward J. Carnell	Inspiration guarantees only an accurate reproducing of the sources that the Scripture writer employed but not a correcting of them. Thus if the source contained an erroneous reference, the Scripture writer recorded that error just as it was in the source. For example, the Chronicler could have been relying on a fallible and erroneous source in drawing up his list of numbers of chariots and horsemen.
The Biblical Errancy Approach* Dewey Beegle	The Bible contains errors—real and insoluble problems. They should be accepted rather than explained away. The nature of inspiration should be inferred from what the Bible has produced. Whatever inspiration is, it is not verbal. Inspiration cannot be regarded as extending to the very choice of words in the text. Therefore, it is not possible or necessary to reconcile all discrepancies.

—— M O R E   I N D U C T I V E →

*These are merely names chosen to distinguish the views. Neither Carnell nor Beegle called their views by the names given here.
Chart is adapted from Gleason L. Archer, "Alleged Errors and Discrepancies in the Original Manuscripts of the Bible," in Norman L. Geisler, ed., *Inerrancy* (Grand Rapids: Zondervan, 1979), pp. 57-82; and Millard J. Erickson, *Christian Theology* (Grand Rapids: Baker, 1983, 1984, 1985), pp. 230-32. Both books are used by permission.

12. Answers to Supposed Discrepancies in Scripture

The following chart reflects a summation of the response given by Gleason L. Archer to alleged errors and discrepancies in Scripture as set forth by William LaSor and Dewey Beegle.* These are considered to be the most difficult of the many discrepancies alleged by critics against the original manuscripts of the Bible. LaSor set forth ten objections, only six of which are charted here because two were answered with one response, one was withdrawn, and two of his objections were leveled at another person's reason rather than at Scripture itself. Beegle set forth eleven objections. Archer addressed only ten of them since the eleventh was a repetition of an area that also concerned LaSor. In regard to the allegations, the obvious intent of this chart is simply to identify the areas of concern and not to provide a full summary of the allegations. This may be obtained by reference to the sources used for the chart.

Alleged Error or discrepancy	Explanation
Numerical Discrepancies in Historical Books 2 Sam. 10:18 vs. 1 Chron. 19:18 2 Chron. 36:9 vs. 2 Kings. 24:8 1 Kings. 4:26 vs. 2 Chron. 9:25 1 Chron. 11:11 vs. 2 Sam. 23:8 LaSor	There is no proof that this discrepancy existed in original manuscripts. It was probably difficult to make out numerals when copying from earlier worn-out manuscripts. Ancient systems of numerical notation were susceptible to mistakes, e.g., leaving off or adding zeros.
Genealogies of Christ Matt. 1 vs. Luke 3 LaSor	It was understood by church fathers that Matthew gives the line of Joseph, the legal father of Jesus, whereas Luke gives the lineage of Mary, his mother. This interpretation goes back to the fifth Christian century, if not earlier.
The Location of Joseph's Grave Acts 7:16 vs. Josh. 24:32 LaSor and Beegle	The parallel case of Isaac confirming with Abimelech his rights to the land where the well of Beersheba was dug (Gen. 26:26-33). The land had been bought earlier by Abraham (21:22-31). Because of the nomadic habits of Abraham, Isaac found it necessary to reestablish his rights to the well. Jacob's buying the burial field near Shechem (33:18-20) was probably a similar situation. Although there is no mention in Genesis of Abraham's buying the land, Stephen probably knew of it by oral tradition; and it is significant that Shechem was the region where Abraham built his first altar after migrating to the Holy Land.

Chart is adapted from Gleason L. Archer, "Alleged Errors and Discrepancies in the Original Manuscripts of the Bible," in Norman L. Geisler, ed., *Inerrancy* (Grand Rapids: Zondervan, 1979), pp. 57-82; and Millard J. Erickson, *Christian Theology* (Grand Rapids: Baker, 1983, 1984, 1985), pp. 230-32. Both books are used by permission.

12. Answers to Supposed Discrepancies (continued)

The Number of Angels at Jesus' Tomb Matt. 28:25; Mark. 16:5 vs. Luke 24:4; John 20:12 LaSor	A careful comparison of the accounts shows that two angels were involved, although the one angel that performed the miracles of the earthquake, rolled back the stone, frightened away the guards, and spoke to the three women at their first approach was probably the more prominent of the two, thus leading Matthew and Mark to refer to him specifically. Parallel instances occur in the Gospels regarding demons (Matt. 8:28 vs. Mark 5:2; Luke 8:27) and blind men (Matt. 20:30 vs. Mark 10:46; Luke 18:35) where the prominence of one being in each instance led some authors to record the presence of just that one being when there were actually two. "One" is different from "one and *only one*."
The Source of the Potters' Field Reference Matt. 27:9 LaSor	Although Matthew quotes partially from Zechariah 11:13, the main point of Matthew's passage (27:6-9) refers to the potter's *field*, which is not mentioned in Zechariah but is in Jeremiah (19:2, 11; 32:9). It was the general practice of New Testament writers, when blending together quotes from Old Testament authors as Matthew was doing here, to refer only to the one who was the more famous. Thus Matthew attributed the quote to Jeremiah. This can be compared with Mark. 1:2-3, where a conflate quotation from Malachi 3:1 and Isaiah 40:3 is attributed only to Isaiah.
Dating of the Exodus Exod. 1:11 vs. I Kings 6:1 LaSor	Judges 11:26 and Acts 13:19 support the 1 Kings. 6:1 claim that the Exodus occurred about 1446 B.C. Biblical and archaeological evidence shows that Exodus 1:11 is not strong evidence for dating the Exodus at 1290 B.C. For Archer's explanation of both these statements, see pages 64-65.
Jude's Reference to Enoch Jude 14 Beegle	Archer points out that there is no reason why pseudepigraphical works written in the intertestamental period, e.g., the *Book of Enoch*, which Jude 14 draws from, may not have included some facts and reports that were historically accurate. Archer argues that Enoch's prophecy was able to be preserved even as Adam and Eve's dialogue was preserved for Moses to record thousands of years later.
Jude's Reference to Michael and Satan Jude 9 Beegle	Beegle's underlying assumption that Jude had no other valid source of information but the Hebrew text of the Old Testament, which does not record this incident, is wrong because Jude's writing was inspired by the Holy Spirit. Actions or statements referred to in Holy Scripture do not have to appear more than once in the Bible in order to be trusted. Beegle, himself, holds John 3:16 to be authentic and trustworthy, even though it occurs only once in the Bible.

12. Answers to Supposed Discrepancies (continued)

Length of Pekah's Reign 2 Kings 15:27 Beegle	Although Pekah was confined to Gilead for the first 12 years of his reign, he was the only legitimate king of Israel from 752 to 732 B.C. The reigns of Menahem and his son Pekahiah from 752 to 740 B.C. were usurpations. Even while confined to Gilead, Pekah claimed the throne to Israel and regarded Samaria as his rightful capital. Parallels are found with David, who is said in 1 Kings. 2:11 to have reigned over Israel for 40 years even though his authority was limited for the first 7 years. King Thutmose III of the Egyptian 18th Dynasty had an official reign of 48-49 years, but since he acceded to the throne as an infant, his stepmother took authority for several years, and Thutmose's effective reign was only 35 years.
Dating of Sennacherib's Invasions 2 Kings 18:1 vs. 2 Kings 18:13 Beegle	No convincing case can be made for a mistake in the original manuscript as a scribal error was obviously made in transcribing 2 Kings 18:13. Whether numerals were used or the numbers were spelled out, 24 could easily be transcribed 14. All other datings in 2 Kings (15:30; 16:1-2; 17:1) support the dating of 18:1. A simple textual correction in 18:13 would harmonize all accounts.
The Number of Rooster Crows at the Time of Peter's Denial Matt. 26:34, 74-75; Luke 22:34, 60-61 vs. Mark 14:30, 72 Beegle	Matthew and Luke at best merely *imply* only one crowing, while Mark specifically mentions two crowings of the rooster. Exegesis confirms that Matthew and Luke do not specify how many times the rooster would crow, and therefore there is no contradiction.
Paul's Quoting of Eliphaz 1 Cor. 3:19 Beegle	It has probably never been claimed by any evangelical scholar that the Bible quotes as valid only the statements of inspired saints or that all statements by these saints are valid. Some of the reproaches that Job directed against God were less than inspired, and for these he was rightly rebuked (Job 34:1-9; 38:1-2; 40:2). On the other hand, many of the sentiments addressed by his three counselors were doctrinally correct. Paul's quotation from Eliphaz poses no threat.
The Leading of David to Take the Census 2 Sam. 24:1 vs. 1 Chron. 21:1 Beegle	The Bible tells us that God may permit a believer who is out of fellowship with Him to take an action that is unwise or displeasing to God in order that, after that person reaps the bitter fruit of his misdeed, he will undergo appropriate disciplinary judgment and thereby be brought back, chastened in the Spirit, to a closer fellowship with the Lord. Such was the case with Jonah. In the latter part of David's reign, he and the nation began to be confident in their increasing numbers and material resources to such an extent that they needed disciplinary judgment to bring them back to proper dependence on God. The Lord therefore permitted Satan to encourage David to undertake the census, which resulted in severe discipline by God. So, both accounts are true, for both God and Satan influenced David.

12. Answers to Supposed Discrepancies (continued)

The Time Span of Genesis 5 and 10 Genealogies Beegle	There is no reason why there cannot be gaps in this genealogy as Luke 3:36 indicates at least one gap in the genealogy found in Genesis 10:24. Also, a careful study of the actual usages of the Hebrew and Greek terms for "father" and "begat" reveals that they often signified nothing more definite than direct line of ancestry; e.g., Jesus was often addressed as "Son of David." Furthermore, neither Genesis 5 nor Genesis 10 mentions any specific time period that totals up the entire span from Adam to Noah or from Noah to Abraham. But the years are given for each generation so that the total time span from Adam to Abraham can be easily ascertained. The problem is tying the biblical chronology into secular historical chronology.
The Age of Terah When Abraham Left Haran Gen. 12:4 vs. Acts 7:4 in light of Gen. 11:26, 32 Beegle	Beegle's inference that Terah was 70 years old when Abraham was born is highly debatable. Scripture says only that Terah was 70 when he had his first son. It does not specifically say who was born first. Abraham was mentioned first probably because of his prominence. Other Scriptures, e.g., Genesis 11:28 indicates that Haran could have been the oldest, since he was the first to die. So there is no difficulty in supposing Abraham was born when Terah was 130 years old. That advanced age for paternity was not unusual at that time.
Jacob's Burial Place Gen. 23:19; 50:13 vs. Acts 7:16 Beegle	When properly exegeted, Acts 7:16 is found to refer to the burial place of Jacob's sons, whereas Genesis 23:19 and 50:13 refer to the burial place of Jacob.
Length of Israelite Sojourn in Egypt Exod. 12:40 vs. Gal. 3:17 Beegle	The thrust of Paul's remark is not to reveal the time period between Genesis 12, when the promise was first given to Abraham, and Exodus 20, when the law was given to Moses. The issue in his statement is that the law, which was given 430 years later than the time of the *three* patriarchs to whom the promises came, was never intended to annul or supersede those promises. Paul simply mentions the well-known interval of the Egyptian sojourn as separating the period of covenant promise and the period of Mosaic legislation. As such, Paul's comment was perfectly historical and accurate.

13. Competing Views of God

View	Polytheism	Idealism
Adherents	Ancient nature religions Hinduism Zen Buddhism Mormonism	Josiah Royce William Hocking Christian Scientists Plato Hegel Emerson
Synthesis of Doctrine	The belief that there is a plurality of gods. Some say it arose as a rejection of monotheism. Often closely tied to nature worship. It is the popular counterpart of pantheism.	This philosophy is a mentalistic reductionism that explains a perceived dualism of matter and mind in terms of one all-inclusive infinite mind. All components of the universe, including good and evil, become but a finite counterpart of the Infinite. All elements merge with the ultimate good. The good in turn represents ideal reality.
View of God	God is relegated to one among many in a pantheon of gods. This differs from henotheism, which, while recognizing many gods, sees one god above the rest.	God is a nebulous embodiment of the Absolute. Though perfect, immutable, and transcendent, he is impersonal.
Scriptural Contrasts	There is only one true God (Deut 6:4; Isa 43:10-11; 1 Cor. 8:4-6; Gal. 4:8).	God is personal as well as transcendent (Ps.103:13; 113:5-6; Isa. 55:8-9). Man is naturally *alienated* from God (Eph. 4:18).

13. Competing Views of God (continued)

View	Realism	Pantheism
Adherents	Thomas Reid Neo–Realists	Spinoza Radhakrishnan Hindus Transcendentalists
Synthesis of Doctrine	Universals have an existence that is in some sense independent of the particular perceptions of the mind. In its pure form, it is diametrically opposed to reductionism. It attempts to balance objectivity and subjectivity. Its systematized framework emphasizes the importance of intuition. It provides a basis for the subject/object distinction.	This view emphasizes God's identity with everything. Reality is pictured as an amorphous fusion of all matter and spirit. Personal being is swallowed up in the one predominant Over-Soul. As such, this view is the polar opposite of deism.
View of God	This view is essentially the same as Idealism. God is distinct from his creation, therefore he transcends it.	God equals everything and everything equals God (God is impersonal and immanent but not transcendent).
Scriptural	See Idealism for the first three points. Man is in no sense independent of God nor can he arrive at spiritual truth independently (Acts 17:28; 1 Cor. 2:10-14).	God is personal and transcendent (Ps. 103:13; 113:5-6; Isa. 55:8-9). Man is a real entity (Gen 2:7; 1 Thess 5:23) and a limited free moral agent (Rom 7:18 with John 6:44).

13. Competing Views of God (continued)

View	Panentheism	Deism
Adherents	Diogenes Henri Bergson Charles Hartshorne Alfred N. Whitehead Schubert Ogden John Cobb	Voltaire Thomas Hobbes Charles Blount John Toland Theistic Evolutionists Thomas Jefferson
Synthesis of Doctrine	A processive view of reality and God (as opposed to a static view) in which a finite God who prehends all the possibilities of the world is gradually actualized in the world in partnership with man. God has a potential pole and an actual pole, hence the term bipolartheism is sometimes used.	Nature and reason point to certain basic truths. By a rational process man can arrive at an understanding of these self-evident truths without the need of divine illumination. This view acknowledges God but denies supernatural intervention in the universe.
View of God	God is finite, distinct from the world, but inseparable from and interdependent with the world.	God is personal and transcendent but not *immanent*. He is a sort of "remote control" God. (He "pushed a button" to create everything and now passively watches what happens.)
Scriptural Contrasts	God is infinite (Ps. 139:7-12; Jer. 23:23; Rev. 1:8). God is transcendent (Ps. 113:5-6). God is omnipotent (Gen. 18:14; Matt 28:18). Man needs God (Acts 17:28). God does not need man (*aseity*: "I am that I am," Exod. 3:14. See also Dan. 4:35).	God is immanent (2 Chron. 16:9; Acts 17:28; Hag. 2:5; Matt. 6:25-30; Acts 17:28). Man is inherently depraved (Jer. 17:9; Eph. 2:1-2) and needs grace to be saved (Eph. 2:8-9). Man is not "autonomous."

14. Seven Major Worldviews

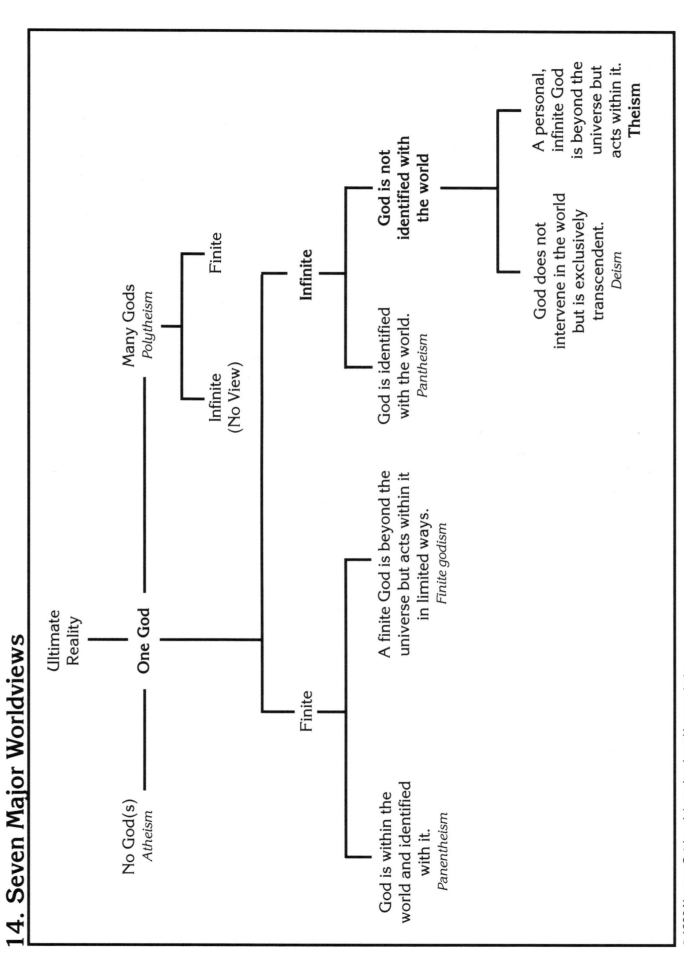

Ultimate Reality

No God(s)
Atheism

One God

Many Gods
Polytheism

Finite

Infinite
(No View)

Finite

Infinite

God is within the world and identified with it.
Panentheism

A finite God is beyond the universe but acts within it in limited ways.
Finite godism

God is identified with the world.
Pantheism

God is not identified with the world

God does not intervene in the world but is exclusively transcendent.
Deism

A personal, infinite God is beyond the universe but acts within it.
Theism

15. Classic Arguments for the Existence of God

Type of Argument	Title of Argument	Proponent of Argument	Content of Argument
a posteriori*	The Argument From Motion	Thomas Aquinas	There is motion (locomotion) in the universe. Something cannot move itself, an external agent or force is required. An infinite regress of forces is meaningless. Hence, there must be a being who is the ultimate source of all motion while not being moved itself. This being is God, the unmoved mover.
a posteriori	The Cosmological Argument (The Argument From Cause)	Thomas Aquinas	Every effect has a cause. There cannot be an infinite regress of finite causes. Therefore, there must be an uncaused cause or necessary being. This being is God.
a posteriori	The Argument From Possibility and Necessity	Thomas Aquinas	Things exist in a network of relationships to other things. They can exist only within this network. Therefore, each is a dependent thing. However, an infinite regress of dependencies is contradictory. There must, then, be a being who is absolutely independent, not contingent on anything else. This being is God.
a posteriori	The Argument From Perfection	Thomas Aquinas	It can be observed in the universe that there is a pyramid of beings (e.g., from insects to man), in an ever-increasing degree of perfection. There must be a final being who is absolutely perfect, the source of all perfection. This being is God.
a posteriori	The Teleological Argument (The Argument From Design)	Thomas Aquinas	There is an observable order or design in the world that cannot be attributed to the object itself (e.g., inanimate objects). This observable order argues for an intelligent being who established this order. This being is God.
a posteriori	The Moral (or Anthropological) Argument	Immanuel Kant	All people possess a moral impulse or categorical imperative. Since this morality is not always rewarded in this life, there must be some basis or reason for moral behavior that is beyond this life. This implies the existence of immortality, ultimate judgment, and a God who establishes and supports morality by rewarding good and punishing evil.
a priori†	The Argument That God Is an Innate Idea	Augustine John Calvin Charles Hodge	Every normal person is born with the idea of God implanted in his mind, though it is suppressed in unrighteousness (Rom. 1:18). As the child grows into adulthood, this idea becomes clearer. Critical experiences in the course of life may make this idea come alive.

34

*a posteriori: statements or arguments that are logically posterior to, or dependent on, sense experience.
†a priori: statements or arguments that are logically prior to, or independent of, sense experience.

15. Classic Arguments (continued)

Type of Argument	Title of Argument	Proponent of Argument	Content of Argument
a priori	The Argument From Mysticism	Evelyn Underhill	Man is able to have a direct mystical experience with God resulting in an ecstatic experience. This union with God is so uniquely overpowering that it self-validates the existence of God.
a priori	The Argument From Truth	Augustine A. H. Strong	All people believe that something is true. If God is the God of truth and the true God, then God is Truth. This Truth (capital T) is the context for all other truth. Therefore, the existence of truth implies the existence of Truth, which implies the existence of God.
a priori	The Ontological Argument	Anselm of Canterbury	Major premise: Man has an idea of an infinite and perfect being. Minor premise: Existence is a necessary part of perfection. Conclusion: An infinite and perfect being exists, since the very concept of perfection requires existence.
a priori	The Argument From Man's Finitude	Aristotle	Man is aware of his finitude. What makes man aware of this? God is continually impressing man with God's infinitude. Therefore the sense of finitude itself is proof that an infinite being, God, exists.
a priori	The Argument From Blessedness	Augustine Thomas Aquinas	Man is restless. He has a vague longing for blessedness. This longing was given by God, for man is restless until he rests in God. The presence of this longing is an indirect proof of God's existence.
a priori	The Argument From Perception	Bishop Berkeley	Man is able to perceive (sense) things around him. This cannot be caused either by physical events (perception as a mental act) or by man himself. Therefore, the existence of perception implies God's existence as the only rational explanation for man's perceptions.
a priori	The Existential Argument	Auguste Sabatier	God proves himself via the Kerygma, which is his declaration of love, forgiveness, and justification of man. When one decides for the Kerygma, he then knows God exists. No other evidence is needed. God is not so much proven as he is known, and this occurs existentially.

16. Evaluation of the Classic Arguments for the Existence of God

The Cosmological Argument

Every effect has a cause; there cannot be an infinite regress of finite causes; therefore, there must be an uncaused cause or necessary being; this being is God.

Proponent
Thomas Aquinas

Arguments For	Arguments Against
The absence of an essential being or uncaused cause ultimately leads to self-creation or chance-creation, both of which are logically impossible.	There is no necessary connection (logically) between cause and effect. At best, we have only a psychological disposition to expect the effect to occur.
A circle or chain of causes would require a link in the chain to be causing existence and having its existence caused simultaneously, potentiality producing actuality, and this is not possible. Nothing cannot cause something.	A circle of causes may be an alternative to an infinite regress of causes.
A necessary being must be infinite. Only that which has potentiality can be limited, and a necessary being must be pure actuality (or else it could be possible for it not to exist).	The existence of an infinite Creator cannot be demonstrated from the existence of a finite universe.
The law of causality applies only to finite beings. God, who is infinite and eternally self-existent, does not require a cause.	If everything needs a cause, so does God, or else God must be self-caused, which is impossible.

The Teleological Argument

There is observable order or design in the world that cannot be attributed to the object itself (e.g. inanimate objects); this observable order argues for an intelligent being who established this order; this being is God.

Proponent
Thomas Aquinas

Arguments For	Arguments Against
Creation by chance is equivalent to self-creation, for chance is a mathematical abstraction with no real existence in and of itself. Also, chance and eternity do not enhance the argument, since in a purely random arena things become more disorganized with time, not less.	The order in the world can be attributed to agents other than an intelligent being, such as chance or natural selection.
Even in what appear to be random natural occurrences and in diseases order is still present. The thrust of this argument is for the *existence* of an intelligent designer. It does *not* try to argue for the *character* of the disigner.	This argument fails to account for occurrences such as natural catastrophes and disease, which argue against the existence of a good God.
This argument is a posteriori–from something outward, i.e., based upon observation. In view of the only alternative basis for postulating intelligent being the a priori–from something inward–we have little choice but to base our arguments for God's existence on what we have observed in the world around us.	This argument is invalid, because it extends the observable to that which goes beyond experience.

16. Evaluation of the Classic Arguments (continued)

The Anthropological (Moral) Argument

All men possess a moral impulse or categorical (moral) imperative. Since this morality is not always rewarded in this life, there must be some basis or reason for moral behavior that is beyond this life. This implies the existence of immortality, ultimate judgment, and a God who establishes and supports morality by rewarding good and punishing evil.

Proponent
Immanuel Kant

Arguments For	Arguments Against
Since man's conscience or moral impulse is often not in his best interests in terms of survival, it is unlikely that it would develop as a necessary part of natural selection.	Man's moral impulse may be attributed to sources other than God, such as the idea of conscience developing as a necessary part of the evolutionary process or of natural selection.
Though the existence of a God who is good (and all-powerful) may mandate the destruction of evil, it does not necessarily mandate that destruction now.	If God exists as a rewarder of good, why does evil exist (especially if, as theists profess, God is all-good *and* all-powerful)?
This moral impulse is based on God's nature, not his arbitrary will. Indeed, God cannot be considered arbitrary, because he cannot will contrary to his nature.	If this moral impulse comes from God's fiat alone, it is arbitrary and God is not essentially good (this militates against the good God of theism, for which this argument is used as proof).

The Ontological Argument

This argument takes the following form (and many others):
- major premise: Man has an idea of an infinite and perfect being.
- minor premise: Existence is a necessary part of perfection.
- conclusion: An infinite and perfect being exists, since the very concept of perfection requires existence.

Proponent
Anselm of Canterbury

Arguments For	Arguments Against
If the statement "no statements about existence are necessary" is true, it must also apply to the statement itself, which would be self-defeating. Hence, it is *possible* that some necessary statements about existence can be made.	Statements about existence cannot be necessary, because necessity is merely a logical characteristic of propositions
	There is no connection between the existence of a perfect being in a person's mind and the actual existence of that being in the world.
	The argument requires an adoption of a Platonic framework, in which the ideal is more real than the physical.

17. Knowledge of God

Natural Revelation	Special Revelation
Given to All Intended for All	Given to Few Intended for All
Sufficient for Condemnation	Sufficient for Salvation
Declares God's Greatness	Declares God's Grace
Loci 1. Nature Psalm 19:1 2. History Israel 3. Human Moral Consciousness 4. Man's Religious Nature	Loci 1. Moses & Prophets Heb. 1:1 2. Incarnation Heb. 1:2 3. Apostles Heb. 2:3-4
Apologetics 1. Cosmological Argument 2. Teleological Argument 3. Anthropological Argument 4. Ontological Argument	Nature 1. Personal Phil. 3:10 2. Anthropic Human Language 3. Analogical Rom. 5:7-8

18. Schemes of Categorizing the Divine Attributes

Strong	Chafer	Erickson	Mueller	Thiessen
Absolute Attributes	**Personality**	**Attributes of Greatness**	**Negative Attributes**	**Essence of God**
Spirituality, involving Life Personality *Infinity, involving* Self-existence Immutability *Perfection, involving* Truth Love Holiness	*Omniscience* *Sensibility* *Holiness* *Justice* *Love* *Goodness* *Truth* *Will* *Freedom* *Omnipotence*	*Spirituality* *Personality* *Life* *Infinity* *Constancy*	*Unity* *Simplicity* *Immutability* *Infinity* *Eternity* *Omnipresence*	*Spirituality* Immaterial, incorporeal Invisible Alive A person *Self-existence* *Immensity* *Eternity*
Relative Attributes	**Constitutional Attributes**	**Attributes of Goodness**	**Positive Attributes**	**The Attributes of God**
Time and Space, in relation to Eternity Immensity *Creation* Omnipresence Omniscience Omnipotence *Moral Beings* Veracity, Faithfulness Mercy, Goodness Justice, Righteousness	*Simplicity* *Unity* *Infinity* *Eternity* *Immutability* *Omnipresence or immensity* *Sovereignty*	*Moral Purity* Holiness Righteousness Justice *Integrity* Genuineness Veracity Faithfulness *Love* Benevolence Grace Mercy Persistence	*Life* *Knowledge* *Wisdom* *Will* *Holiness* *Justice* *Veracity* *Power* *Goodness*	*Non-moral Attributes* Omnipresence Omniscience Omnipotence Immutability *Moral Attributes* Holiness Righteousness and Justice Goodness Truth

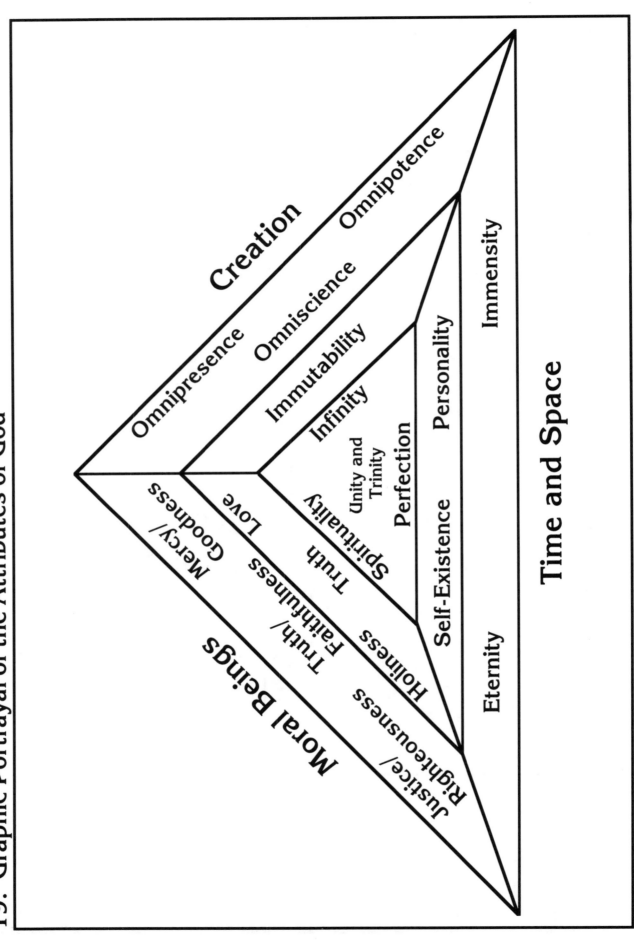

20. Definitions of the Attributes of God

Attribute	Definition	Scripture Reference
Simplicity/ Spirituality	God is uncompounded, incomplex, indivisible, unique, and spirit in essential being.	John 1:18; 4:24; 1 Tim. 1:17; 6:15-16
Unity	God is one.	Deut. 6:4; 1 Cor. 8:6
Infinity	God is without termination and finitude.	1 Kings. 8:27; Ps. 145:3; Acts 17:24
Eternity	God is free from succession of time.	Gen. 21:33; Ps. 90:2
Immutability/ Constancy	God is unchanging and unchangeable in his being.	Ps. 102:27; Mal. 3:6; James 1:17
Omnipresence	God is present everywhere.	Ps. 139:7-12; Jer. 23:23-24
Sovereignty	God is the supreme ruler, independent of any authority outside of himself.	Eph. 1, esp. v. 21
Omniscience	God knows all actual and possible things.	Pss. 139:1-4; 147:4-5; Matt. 11:21
Omnipotence	God is all powerful	Matt. 19:26; Rev. 19:6
Justice	God has moral equity; he does not show favoritism.	Acts 10:34-35; Rom. 2:11
Love	God seeks the highest good of humans at his own infinite cost.	Ps. 103:17; Eph. 2:4-5; 1 John 4:8, 10
Benevolence	God has unselfish concern for the welfare of those he loves.	Deut. 7:7-8; John 3:16
Grace	God supplies those he loves with undeserved favors according to their need.	Exod. 34:6; Eph. 1:5-8; Titus 2:11

20. Definitions of the Attributes of God (continued)

Attribute	Definition	Scripture Reference
Goodness	That which constitutes the character of God and is shown by benevolence, mercy, and grace	Exod. 33:19; Ps. 145:9
Freedom	God is independent from his creatures.	Ps. 115:3
Holiness	God is righteous, perfect, set apart or separate from all sin or evil.	1 Peter 1:16
Righteousness	Holiness applied to relationships; God's law and his actions are exactly right.	Ps. 19:7-9; Jer. 9:24a
Truth	Agreement and consistency with all that is represented by God himself	John 14:6; 17:3
Genuineness	God is real/true.	Jer. 10:5-10; John. 17:3
Veracity	God speaks the truth and is trustworthy.	1 Sam. 15:29; John 17:17, 19; Heb. 6:18; Titus 1:2
Faithfulness	God proves true; he keeps his promises.	Num. 23:19; Ps. 89:2; 1 Thess. 5:24
Personality	God is personal. He has self-cognizance, will, intellect, self-determination.	Exod. 3:14; Gen. 3
Life	God is life and the ultimate source of all of life.	Exod. 3:14; Jer. 10:10; John 5:26
Mercy	God's tenderhearted, showing compassion toward the miserable, needy people he loves and also his not bringing on fallen people what they deserve	Exod. 3:7, 17; Ps. 103:13; Matt. 9:36
Persistence	God's long-suffering nature and his patience toward his people	Ps. 86:15; Rom. 2:4; 9:22

21. Historical Development of the Doctrine of the Trinity

Introduction

The doctrine of the Trinity is central to biblical Christianity; it describes the relationships among the three members of the Godhead in a manner consistent with the Scriptures.

Central to this doctrine is the question of how God can be both one and three. The early Christians did not want to lose their Jewish monotheism while exalting their Savior. Heresies emerged as men sought to explain the Christian God without becoming tritheists (which Jews were quick to accuse them of being). Christians argued that O.T. Jewish monotheism did not preclude the Trinity.

The climax of Trinitarian formulation occurred at the Council of Constantinople in A.D. 381. To this council we owe the expression of the orthodox view of the Trinity. To appreciate what the council said, however, it is helpful to trace the doctrine's historical development. This is not meant to imply that the church or any council invented the doctrine. Rather, it was in response to heresies that the church explicated what the Scriptures already assumed.

The Pre-Nicene Church: A.D. 33-325

The Apostles, A.D. 33-100
Apostolic teaching clearly accepted the full and real deity of Jesus and accepted and adopted the Trinitarian baptismal formula.

The Apostolic Fathers, A.D. 100-150
The writings of the apostolic fathers were marked by passion about Christ (Christ is from God; he is preexistent) and theological ambiguity about the Trinity.

The Apologists and Polemicists, A.D. 150-325
Increasing persecution and heresy forced Christian writers to state more precisely and to defend the biblical teaching concerning God the Father, Son, and Holy Spirit.

> Justin Martyr: Christ is distinct in function from the Father.
>
> Athenagorus: Christ was without beginning.
>
> Theophilus: The Holy Spirit is distinct from the Logos.
>
> Origin: The Holy Spirit is coeternal with the Father and the Son.
>
> Tertullian: He spoke of "trinity" and "persons"–three in number, but one in substance.

21. Doctrine of the Trinity (continued)

The Council of Nicea: A.D. 325

Because of the spread of the Arian heresy, which denied the deity of Christ, the unity and even the future of the Roman Empire seemed uncertain. The newly converted Constantine convened an ecumenical council in Nicea to settle the issue.

The Issue: Was Christ fully God, or was he a created and subordinate being?

Arius	Athanasius
Only God the Father is eternal.	Christ is co-eternal with the Father.
The Son had a beginning as the first and highest created being.	Christ had no beginning.
The Son is not one in essence with the Father.	The Son and Father are of the same essence.
Christ is subordinate to the Father.	Christ is not subordinate to the Father.
He is called God as an honorific title.	

Crucial Statements of the Council's Creed

[We believe] "in one Lord Jesus Christ . . . true God of true God, not made, of one substance with the Father."

"But those who say there was when He was not, and before being begotten He was not . . . these the Catholic Church anathematizes."

"And we believe in the Holy Spirit."

Results From the Council

Arianism was formally condemned.

The *homoousia* (same substance) statement created conflicts.

Arians reinterpreted *homoousia* and accused the council of modalistic monarchianism.

Doctrine of the Holy Spirit was left undeveloped.

The Council of Constantinople: A.D. 381

Arianism was not extinguished at Nicea; it actually grew in prominence. Additionally, Macedonianism emerged, which subordinated the Holy Spirit in much the same manner as Arianism had subordinated Christ.

The Issue: Is the Holy Spirit fully God?

Crucial Statement of the Council's Creed

". . . and in the Holy Spirit, the Lord and life-giver, who proceeds from the Father, who is worshiped and glorified together with the Father and the Son."

Results From the Council

Arianism was rebuffed and the Nicene Creed reaffirmed.

Macedonianism was condemned and Holy Spirit's deity affirmed.

Major conflicts over Trinitarianism were resolved (though Christological debates continued until Chalcedon, A.D. 451).

22. Ancient Diagram of the Holy Trinity

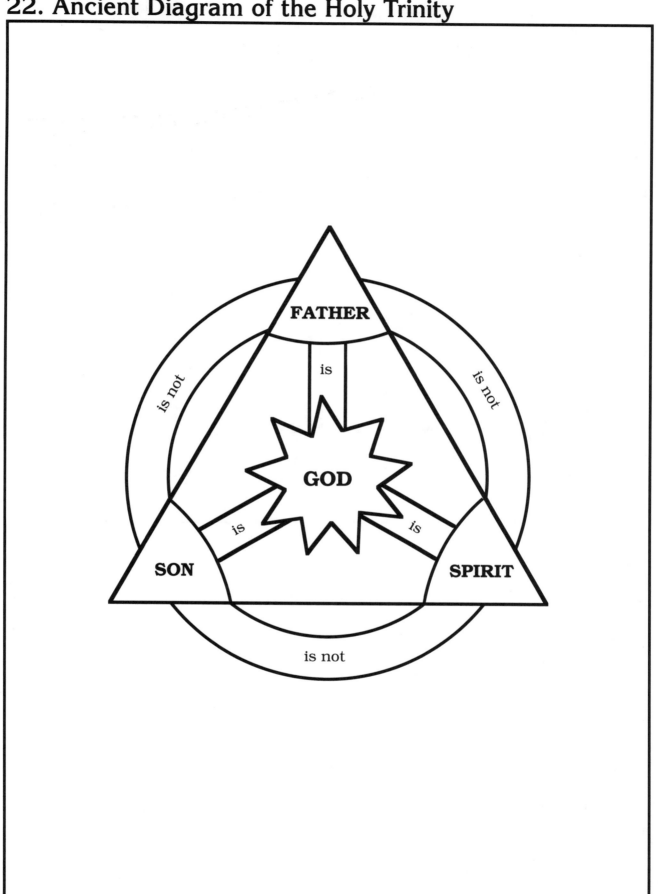

23. Major Views of the Trinity

View	Source	Adherents	Perception of God's Essence (Oneness-Unity)	Perception of God's Subsistence (Threeness-Diversity)
Dynamic Monarchianism	Theodotus	Paul of Samosata Artemon Socinius Modern Unitarians	The unity of God denotes both oneness of nature and oneness of *person*. The Son and the Holy Spirit therefore are consubstantial with the Father's divine essence only as impersonal *attributes*. The divine *dunamis* came upon the man Jesus, but he was not God in the strict sense of the word.	The notion of a subsistent God is a palpable impossibility, since his perfect unity is perfectly indivisible. The 'diversity' of God is apparent and not real, since the Christ event and the work of the Holy Spirit attest only to a dynamic operation within God, not to a hypostatic union.
Modalistic Monarchianism	Praxeas	Noaetus Sabellius Swedenborg Schleiermacher United Pentecostals (Jesus Only)	The unity of God is ultra-simplex. He is qualitatively characterized in his essence by one nature and one person. This essence may be designated interchangeably as Father, Son, and Holy Spirit. They are different names *for* but identical *with* the unified, simplex God. The three names are the three modes by which God reveals himself.	The concept of a subsistent God is erroneous and confounds the real issue of the phenomenon of God's modalistic manifestation of himself. The paradox of a subsisting "three in oneness" is refuted by recognizing that God is not three persons but one person with three different names and corresponding roles following one another like parts of a drama.
Subordinationism	Arius	Modern Jehovah's Witnesses and several other lesser known cults	The inherent oneness of God's nature is properly identifiable with the Father only. The Son and the Holy Spirit are discrete entities who do not share the divine essence.	The unipersonal essence of God precludes the concept of divine subsistence with a Godhead. "Threeness in oneness" is self-contradictory and violates the biblical principles of a monotheistic God.
"Economic" Trinitarianism	Hippolytus Tertullian	Various "neo-economic" Trinitarians	The Godhead is characterized by triunity: Father, Son, and Holy Spirit are three manifestations of one identical, indivisible substance. The perfect unity and consubstantiality are especially comprehended in such manifest Triadic deeds as creation and redemption.	Subsistence within the Godhead is articulated by means of such terms as "distinction" and "distribution," dispelling effectively the notion of separateness or division.
Orthodox Trinitarianism	Athanasius	Basil Gregory of Nyssa Gregory of Nazianzus Augustine Thomas Aquinas Luther Calvin Contemporary orthodox Christianity	God's being is perfectly unified and simplex: of one essence (*homoousia*). This essence of deity is held in common by Father, Son, and Holy Spirit. The three persons are consubstantial, coinherent (*perichoresis*), co-equal, and co-eternal.	The divine subsistence is said to occur simultaneously in three modes of being or hypostases. As such, the Godhead exists "undivided in divided persons." This view contemplates an *identity* in nature and *cooperation* in function without the denial of the distinctions of persons in the Godhead.

23. Major Views of the Trinity (continued)

View	Asignation of Deity/Eternality			Analogical Referent(s)	Criticism(s)
	Father	Son	Holy Spirit		
Dynamic Monarchianism	Unique Originator of the universe. He is eternal, self-existent, and without beginning or end.	A virtuous (but finite) man in whose life God was dynamically present in a unique way; Christ definitely was *not* deity though his humanity was deified..	An impersonal attribute of the Godhead. No deity/or eternality is ascribed to the Holy Spirit.		Elevates reason above the witness of biblical revelation concerning the Trinity. Categorically denies the deity of Christ and of the Holy Spirit, thereby undermining the theological underginding for the biblical doctrine of salvation.
Modalistic Monarchianism	Fully God and fully eternal as the primal mode or manifestation of the only unique and unitary God.	Full deity/eternality ascribed only in the sense of his being another mode of the one God and identical with his essence. He is the same God manifested in *temporal sequence* specific to a role (incarnation).	Eternal God only as the title designates the *phase* in which the one God, in *temporal sequence, manifested* himself pursuant to the role of regeneration and sanctification.	One person acting three different roles in the same drama. Water-ice-vapor	Depersonalizes the Godhead. To compensate for its Trinitarian deficiencies, this view propounds ideas that are clearly heretical (e.g., patripassianism). Its concept of successive manifestations of the Godhead cannot account for such simultaneous appearances of the three persons as at Christ's baptism.
Subordinationism	The only one, unbegotten God who is eternal and without beginning	A created being and therefore not eternal. Though he is to be venerated, he is not of the divine essence.	A nonpersonal, noneternal emanation of the Father. He is viewed as an influence, an expression of God. Deity is not ascribed to him.	Mind-idea-action	It is at variance with abundant scriptural testimony respecting the deity of both Christ and the Holy Spirit. Its hierarchical concept likewise asserts three essentially separate persons with regard to the Father, Christ, and Holy Spirit. This results in a totally confused soteriology.
"Economic" Trinitarianism	The equal deity of Father, Son, and Holy Spirit is clearly elucidated in observation of the simultaneous relational/operational features of the Godhead. Co-eternality, at times, does not intelligibly surface in this ambiguous view, but it seems to be a logical implication.			A source and its river. Unity between a root and its shoot. The sun and its light.	Is more tentative and ambiguous in its treatment of the relational aspect of the Trinity.
Orthodox Trinitarianism	In its final distillation, this view unhesitatingly sets forth Father, Son, and Holy Spirit as co-equal and co-eternal in the Godhead with regard to both the divine essence and function.			All analogies fail to express orthodox Trinitarianism adequately.	The only shortcoming has to do with the limitations inherent in human language and thought itself: the impossibility of totally describing the ineffable mystery of "three in oneness."

24. A Biblical Presentation of the Trinity

Introduction	The word "Trinity" is never used, nor is the doctrine of Trinitarianism ever explicitly taught in the Scriptures, but Trinitarianism is the best explication of the biblical evidence. The theological exposition of the doctrine arose from clear, but not comprehensive, scriptural teaching. It is a crucial doctrine for Christianity because it focuses on who God is, and particularly on the deity of Jesus Christ. Because Trinitarianism is not taught explicitly in the Scriptures, the study of the doctrine is an exercise in putting together biblical themes and data through a systematic theological study and through looking at the historical development of the present orthodox view of what the biblical presentation of the Trinity is.	
Essential Elements of the Trinity	1. God is One. 2. Each of the persons within the Godhead is Deity. 3. The oneness of God and the threeness of God are not contradictory. 4. The Trinity (Father, Son, and Holy Spirit) is eternal. 5. Each of the persons of God is of the same essence and is not inferior or superior to the others in essence. 6. The Trinity is a mystery which we will never be able to understand fully.	
Biblical Teaching	**Old Testament**	**New Testament**
God is One	Hear, O Israel: The LORD our God, the LORD is one (Deut 6:4; cf. 20:2-3; 3:13-15).	Now to the King eternal, immortal, invisible, the only God, be honor and glory for ever and ever. Amen (1 Tim . 1:17; cf. 1 Cor. 8:4-6; 1 Tim. 2:5-6; James 2:19).
Three Distinct Persons as Deity	The Father: He said to me, "You are my Son; today I have become your Father" (Ps. 2:7).	. . . who have been chosen according to the foreknowledge of God the Father . . . (1 Peter 1:2; cf. John 1:17; 1 Cor. 8:6; Phil. 2:11).
	The Son: He said to me, "You are my Son; today I have become your Father" (Ps. 2:7; cf. Heb. 1:1-13; Ps. 68:18; Isa. 6:1-3; 9:6).	As soon as Jesus was baptized, he went up out of the water. At that moment heaven was opened, and he saw the Spirit of God descending like a dove and lighting on him. And a voice from heaven said, "This is my Son, whom I love; with him I am well pleased" (Matt. 3:16-17).
	The Holy Spirit: In the beginning God created the heavens and the earth . . . and the Spirit of God was hovering over the waters (Gen. 1:1-2; cf. Exod. 31:3; Judg. 15:14; Isa. 11:2).	Then Peter said, "Ananias, how is it that Satan has so filled your heart that you have lied to the Holy Spirit . . . ? You have not lied to men but to God" (Acts 5:3-4; cf. 2 Cor. 3:17).

24. A Biblical Presentation of the Trinity (continued)

Plurality of Persons in the Godhead

The use of plural pronouns points to, or at least suggests, the plurality of persons within the Godhead in the Old Testament.

"Then God said, 'Let us make man in our image, in our likeness. . . .'"

The use of the singular word "name" when referring to God the Father, Son, and Holy Spirit indicates a unity within the threeness of God.

"Therefore go and make disciples of all nations, baptizing them in the name of the Father and of the Son and of the Holy Spirit" (Matt. 28:19).

Persons of the Same Essence: Attributes Applied to Each Person

Attribute	Father	Son	Holy Spirit
Eternality	Ps. 90:2	John 1:2; Rev. 1:8, 17	Heb. 9:14
Power	1 Peter 1:5	2 Cor. 12:9	Rom. 15:19
Omniscience	Jer. 17:10	Rev. 2:23	1 Cor. 2:11
Omnipresence	Jer. 23:24	Matt. 18:20	Ps. 139:7
Holiness	Rev. 15:4	Acts 3:14	Acts 1:8
Truth	John 7:28	Rev. 3:7	1 John 5:6
Benevolence	Rom. 2:4	Eph. 5:25	Neh. 9:20

Equality with Different Roles: Activities Involving All Three Persons

Attribute	Father	Son	Holy Spirit
Creation of the World	Ps. 102:25	Col. 1:16	Gen. 1:2; Job 26:13
Creation of Man	Gen. 2:7	Col. 1:16	Job 33:4
Baptism of Christ	Matt. 3:17	Matt. 3:16	Matt. 3:16
Death of Christ	Heb. 9:14	Heb. 9:14	Heb. 9:14

25. False Views of the Trinity

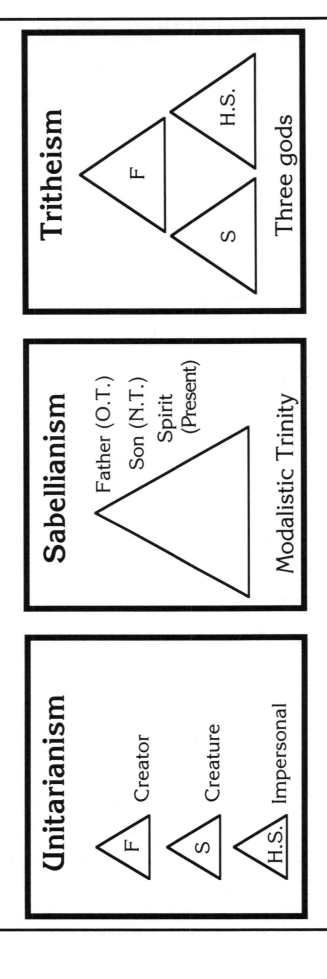

Unitarianism

F Creator

S Creature

H.S. Impersonal

Sabellianism

Father (O.T.)
Son (N.T.)
Spirit (Present)

Modalistic Trinity

Tritheism

F

S   H.S.

Three gods

26. The Names of God

Names	Meaning/Significance	Scripture Reference
Yahweh/Jehovah	The self-existent One. Some think it emphasizes the ontological nature of God: "I AM WHO I AM"; others believe it sets forth the faithfulness of God: "I am [or will be] who I have been," or "I will be who I will be." This name is the personal and proper name for God.	Exod. 3:14-15; cf. Gen. 12:8; 13:4; 26:25; Exod. 6:3; 7; 20:2; 33:19; 34:5-7; Pss. 68:4; 76:1; Jer. 31:31-34
Yahweh Yireh	Yahweh will provide	Gen. 22:8-14
Yahweh Nissi	Yahweh is my banner	Exod. 17:15
Yahweh Shalom	Yahweh is peace	Judg. 6:24
Yahweh Sabbaoth	Yahweh of hosts [armies]	1 Sam. 1:3; 17:45; Ps. 24:10; 46:7, 11
Yahweh Maccaddeshem	Yahweh your sanctifier	Exod. 31:13
Yahweh Raah	Yahweh is my shepherd	Ps. 23:1
Yahweh Tsidkenu	Yahweh our righteousness	Jer. 23:6; 33:16
Yahweh El Gemolah	Yahweh God of recompense	Jer. 51:56
Yahweh Nakeh	Yahweh who smites	Ezek. 7:9
Yahweh Shammah	Yahweh who is present	Ezek. 48:35
Yahweh Rapha	Yahweh who heals	Exod. 15:26
Yahweh Elohim	Yahweh, the Mighty One	Judg. 5:3; Isa. 17:6

26. The Names of God (continued)

Names	Meaning/Significance	Scripture Reference
Adonai	Lord, Master; the name of God used for Yahweh when the proper name of God came to be thought of as too sacred to pronounce	Exod. 4:10-12; Josh. 7:8-11
Elohim	Mighty One; a plural term for God usually speaking of either his majesty or his plenitude	Gen. 1:1, 26-27; 3:5; 31:13; Deut. 5:9; 6:4; Pss. 5:7; 86:15; 100:3
El Elyon	Most High (lit., the strongest Mighty One)	Gen. 14:18; Num. 24:16; Isa. 14:13-14
El Roi	The Mighty One who sees	Gen. 16:13
El Shaddai	Almighty God or All-Sufficient God	Gen. 17:1-20
El Olam	Everlasting God or God of Eternity	Gen. 21:33; Isa. 40:28
El Elohe Israel	God, the God of Israel	Gen. 33:20
Yeshua	Jesus, Yahweh is Savior or Salvation	Matt. 16:13-16; John 6:42; Acts 2:36; Titus 2:13; 2 Peter 1:11
Christos	Christ, Messiah, the Anointed One	Matt. 16:13-16; John 1:41; 20:31; Acts 2:36; Rom. 6:23; Titus 2:13; 2 Peter 1:11
Kurios	Lord, master, sir	Luke 1:46; Acts 2:36; Jude 4
Soter	Savior; one who delivers from danger and death	Luke 1:47; 2:11
Theos	God, a class noun that can refer to any god or to the one true God; used of the Lord Jesus as true God	Luke 1:47; John 20:28; Titus 2:13; 2 Peter 1:11

27. Historical Christological Heresies

Viewpoints of the	Ebionites	Docetists	Arians
Proponents	Judaizers	Basilides Valentinus Patripassians Sabellians	Arius, presbyter of Alexandria Origen (?)
Time	2nd century	Late 1st century	4th century
Denial	Genuine deity	Genuine humanity	Genuine deity
Explanation	Christ had the Spirit after his baptism; he was not preexistent.	Jesus appeared human but was really divine.	Christ was the first and highest created being, *homoiousia*, not *homoousia*.
Condemned	No official condemnation	No official condemnation	Council of Nicea, A.D. 325
Associated with	Legalism	Evil of the material world and oussian divinity of man as taught by Marcion and Gnostics	Generation=creation
Argument for	They are monotheistic.	They affirm Christ's deity	They teach that Christ is subordinate to the Father.
Argument against	Only a divine Christ is worthy of worship (John 1:1; 20:28 Heb. 13:8).	If Christ were not human He could not redeem humanity (Heb. 2:14; 1 John 4:1-3).	Only a divine Christ is worthy of worship; this view tends toward polytheism. Only a divine Christ can save (Phil. 2:6; Rev. 1:8).
Major Opponents	Irenaeus Hippolytus Origen Eusebius	Irenaeus Hippolytus	Athanasius Ossius

27. Historical Christological Heresies (continued)

Viewpoints of the	Appollinarians	Nestorians	Eutychians
Proponents	Appollinarius, bishop of Laodicea Justin Martyr	Represented by Nestorius, 5th-century bishop of Constantinople	Represented by Eutychius Theodosius II
Time	4th century	5th century	5th century
Denial	Completeness of humanity	Unity of person	Distinction of natures
Explanation	The divine Logos took the place of the human mind.	Union was moral, not organic–thus two persons. The human was completely controlled by the divine.	Monophysitist; the human nature was swallowed by the divine to create a new third nature–a *tertium quid.*
Condemned	Council of Antioch, A.D. 378, 379 Council of Constantinople, A.D. 381	Synod of Ephesus, A.D. 431	Council of Chalcedon, A.D. 405; defended by "Robber Synod" of Ephesus, A.D. 449; Condemned by Chalcedon, A.D. 451
Associated with	Logos=reason in all people	"Word-man" (Antiochene) not "word-flesh"(Alexandrian) Christology; opposed to using *theotokos* of Mary.	Concern for the unity and divinity of Christ; Alexandrian (minimized humanity)
Argument for	Affirmed Christ's deity and real humanness.	Distinguished human Jesus, who died, from Divine Son, who cannot die.	Maintained the unity of Christ's person.
Argument against	If Christ did not have a human mind, he would not be truly human (Heb. 2:14; 1 John 4:1-3).	If the death of Jesus was the act of a human person, not of God, it could not be efficacious (Rev. 1:12-18).	If Christ were neither a man nor God, he could not redeem as man or as God (Phil. 2:6).
Major Opponents	Vitalis Pope Damascus Basil, Theodosius Gregory of Nazianzen Gregory of Nyssa	Cyril of Alexandria	Flavian of Constantinople Pope Leo Theodoret Eusebius of Dorylaeum

28. False Views of the Person of Christ

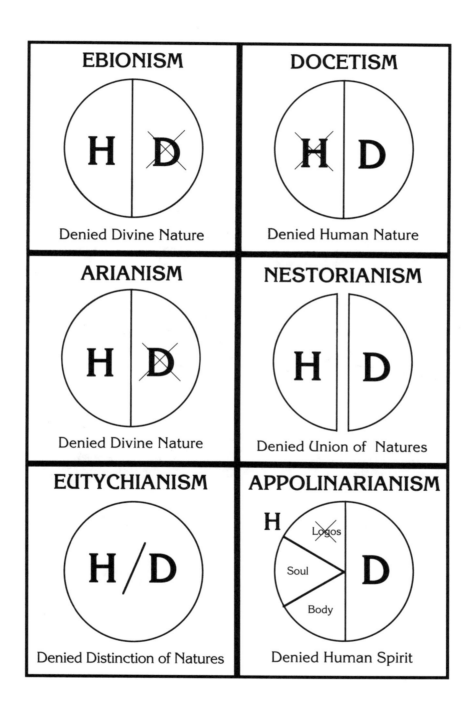

EBIONISM

H | D̶

Denied Divine Nature

DOCETISM

H̶ | D

Denied Human Nature

ARIANISM

H | D̶

Denied Divine Nature

NESTORIANISM

H | D

Denied Union of Natures

EUTYCHIANISM

H/D

Denied Distinction of Natures

APPOLINARIANISM

H

Logos

Soul

Body

D

Denied Human Spirit

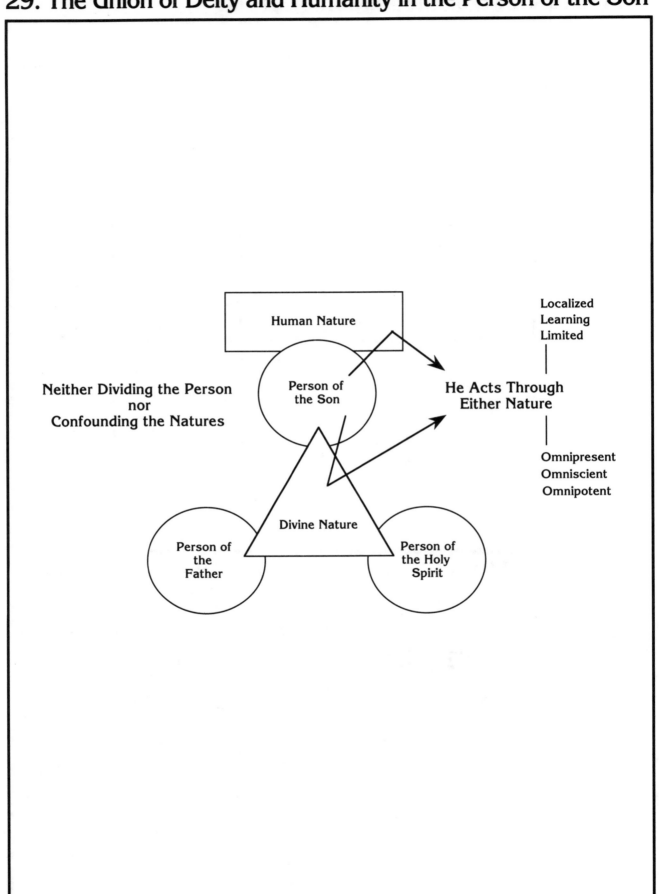

Human Nature

Neither Dividing the Person
nor
Confounding the Natures

Person of
the Son

Localized
Learning
Limited

He Acts Through
Either Nature

Omnipresent
Omniscient
Omnipotent

Divine Nature

Person of
the
Father

Person of
the Holy
Spirit

30. Theories of the Kenosis

Traditional Kenotic Theories	
Christ Emptied Himself of *Divine Consciousness*	The Son of God laid aside his participation in the Godhead when he became a man. All the attributes of his deity literally ceased when the incarnation occurred. The Logos became a soul residing in the human Jesus.
Christ Emptied Himself of the *Eternity Form of Being*	The Logos exchanged his eternity-form for a time-form bound down by human nature. In this time-form Christ no longer had all the attributes commensurate with Deity, though he could use supernatural powers.
Christ Emptied Himself of the *Relative Attributes of Deity*	This view differentiates between essential attributes, such as truth and love, and those that relate to the created universe, such as omnipotence and omnipresence.
Christ Emptied Himself of the *Integrity of Infinite Divine Existence*	At Christ's incarnation the Logos took up a double life. One "life center" continued to function consciously in the Trinity while the other became incarnated with human nature, unaware of the cosmic functions of Deity.
Christ Emptied Himself of the *Divine Activity*	The Logos turned over all of his divine roles and duties to the Father. The incarnate Logos was unaware of the happenings within the Godhead.

Adapted from Robert E. Picirilli, "He Emptied Himself," *Biblical Viewpoint*, Vol. 3, No. 1 (April 1969):23-30. Used by permission.

Christ Emptied Himself of the *Actual Exercise of Divine Prerogatives*	The Logos retracted the mode of the divine attributes from the realm of the actual to the potential. He retained his divine consciousness but renounced the conditions of infinity and its form.

Sub-Kenotic Theories

Christ Emptied Himself of the *Use of the Divine Attributes*	The Logos possessed the divine attributes but chose not to use them.
Christ Emptied Himself of the *Independent Exercise of the Divine Attributes*	The Logos always possessed and could utilize the prerogatives of Deity but always in submission to and by the power of the Father (and the Holy Spirit). The incarnate Christ never did anything independently by virtue of his own deity.
Christ Emptied Himself of the *Insignia of Majesty, the Prerogatives of Deity*	The Logos emptied himself of the outward form of Deity. (This view is vague as to what is precisely meant.)

31. The Person of Christ

Preincarnate	Divine Nature	Human Nature	Union of Natures	Character
Existed Eternally Before Creation From the "beginning" (John 1:1; 1 John 1:1) "With God" (John 1:1-2) "Before the world was" (John 17:5) The Word "became flesh" (implies a preincarnate existence, John 1:14).	**Possesses Divine Attributes** He is eternal (John 1:1; 8:58; 17:5). He is omnipresent (Matt 28:20; Eph. 1:23). He is omniscient (John 16:30; 21:17). He is omnipotent (John 5:19) He is immutable (Heb. 1:12; 13:8)	**Had a Human Birth** He was born of a virgin (Matt 1:18-2:11; Luke 1:30-38). **Had a Human Development** He continued to grow and become strong (Luke 2:50, 52).	**Theanthropic** The person of Christ *is* theanthropic; he has two natures (divine and human in one person). **Personal** Hypostatic union, constituting one personal substance; two natures; one person	**Absolutely Holy** His human nature was created holy (Luke1:35) He committed no sin (1 Peter 2:22). He always pleased the Father (John 8:29).
Participated in Creation "Let *us* make man" (Gen. 1:26). The "craftsman" (Prov. 8:30) The "firstborn over all creation" (Col. 1:15) All things were created "through him" (John 1:3; Col. 1:16). World created "through him" (John 1:10; 1 Cor. 8:6) All things created "for him" (Col. 1:16). All things hold together "in him" (Col. 1:17).	**Possesses Divine Offices** He is Creator (John 1:3; Col. 1:16). He is sustainer (Col. 1:17). **Possesses Divine Prerogatives** He forgives sin (Matt. 9:2; Luke 7:47). He raises the dead (John 5:25;11:25). He executes judgment (John 5:22).	**Had the Essential Elements of Human Nature** Human body (Matt. 26:12; John 2:21) Reason and will (Matt. 26:38; Mark. 2:8) **Had Human Names** Jesus (Matt. 1:21) Son of Man (Matt. 8:20; 11:18) Son of Abraham (Matt. 1:1)	**Includes the Human and Divine Qualities and Acts** Both the human and divine qualities and acts may be ascribed to Jesus Christ under either of his natures.	**Possesses Genuine Love** He laid down his life (John 15:13). His love surpasses all knowledge
Manifested Himself After Creation (Old Testament) As "Yahweh" To Abraham (Gen. 18) In judgment (Gen. 19) In promise (Hos. 1:7) As the "angel of Yahweh" To Hagar (Gen. 16) To Abraham (Gen. 22) To Jacob (Gen. 31) To Moses (Exod. 3:2) To Israel (Exod. 14:19) To Balaam (Num. 22:22) To Gideon (Judg. 6)	**He Is Identified With the Old Testament Yahweh** "I AM" (John 8:58). Seen by Isaiah (John 12:41; 8:24; 50-58) **Possesses Divine Names** "Alpha and the Omega" (Rev. 22:13) "I AM" (John 8:58) "Immanuel" (Matt 1:22) "Son of Man" (Matt. 9:6; 12:8) "Lord" (Matt 7:21; Luke 1:43) "Son of God" (John 10:36) "God" (John 1:1; 2 Peter 1:1) **Possesses Divine Relations** The expressed image of God (Col. 1:15; Heb. 1:3) He is one with the Father (John10:31). **Accepts Divine Worship** (Matt. 14:33; 28:9; John 20:28-29) **Claims Himself to be God** (John 8:58; 10:30;17:5)	**Had the Sinless Infirmities of Human Nature** He became weary (John 4:6). He became hungry (Matt. 4:2; 21:18). He became thirsty (John 19:28). He was tempted (Matt. 4; Heb. 2:18). **Was Repeatedly Called a Man** (John 1:30; 4:9; 10:38)	**Constant Presence of Both Humanity and Divinity** His natures cannot be separated.	**Truly Humble** He took the form of a servant (Phil. 2:5-8). **Thoroughly Meek** (Matt. 11:29) **Perfectly Balanced** He was grave without being melancholy. He was joyful without being frivolous. **Lived a Life of Prayer** (Matt. 14:23; Luke 6:12) **An Incessant Worker** He worked the works of his Father (John. 5:17; 9:4).

32. Messianic Prophecies Fulfilled in Christ

(Presented in the Order of Their Fulfillment)

Scripture Stating Prophecy	Subject of Prophecy	Scripture Stating Fulfillment
Genesis 3:15	Born of the seed of a woman	Galatians 4:4
Genesis 12:2–3	Born of the seed of Abraham	Matthew 1:1
Genesis 17:19	Born of the seed of Isaac	Matthew 1:2
Numbers 24:17	Born of the seed of Jacob	Matthew 1:2
Genesis 49:10	Descended from the tribe of Judah	Luke 3:33
Isaiah 9:7	Heir to the throne of David	Luke 1:32–33
Daniel 9:25	Time for Jesus' birth	Luke 2:1–2
Isaiah 7:14	Born of a virgin	Luke 1:26–27, 30–31
Micah 5:2	Born in Bethlehem	Luke 2:4–7
Jeremiah 31:15	Slaughter of the innocents	Matthew 2:16–18
Hosea 11:1	Flight to Egypt	Matthew 2:14–15
Isaiah 40:3–5; Malachi 3:1	Preceded by a forerunner	Luke 7:24, 27
Psalm 2:7	Declared the Son of God	Matthew 3:16–17
Isaiah 9:1–2	Galilean ministry	Matthew 4:13–17
Deuteronomy 18:15	The prophet to come	Acts 3:20, 22
Isaiah 61:1–2	Came to heal the brokenhearted	Luke 4:18–19
Isaiah 53:3	Rejected by his own (the Jews)	John 1:11
Psalm 110:4	A priest after the order of Melchizedek	Hebrews 5:5–6
Zechariah 9:9	Triumphal entry	Mark 11:7, 9, 11

32. Messianic Prophecies Fulfilled in Christ (continued)

Scripture Stating Prophecy	Subject of Prophecy	Scripture Stating Fulfillment
Psalm 41:9	Betrayed by a friend	Luke 22:47, 48
Zechariah 11:12–13	Sold for thirty pieces of silver	Matthew 26:15; 27:5–7
Psalm 35:11	Accused by false witness	Mark 14:57–58
Isaiah 53:7	Silent to accusations	Mark 15:4, 5
Isaiah 50:6	Spat upon and smitten	Matthew 26:67
Psalm 35:19	Hated without reason	John 15:24, 25
Isaiah 53:5	Vicarious sacrifice	Romans 5:6, 8
Isaiah 53:12	Crucified with transgressors	Mark 15:27, 28
Zechariah 12:10	Hands pierced	John 20:27
Psalm 22:7–8	Scorned and mocked	Luke 23:35
Psalm 69:21	Given vinegar and gall	Matthew 27:34
Psalm 109:4	Prayer for his enemies	Luke 23:34
Psalm 22:18	Soldiers gambled for his coat	Matthew 27:35
Psalm 34:20	No bones broken	John 19:32–33, 36
Zechariah 12:10	Side pierced	John 19:34
Isaiah 53:9	Buried with the rich	Matthew 27:57–60
Psalm 16:10; 49:15	Would rise from the dead	Mark 16:6-7
Psalm 68:18	Would ascend to God's right hand	Mark 16:19

33. The Peccability versus Impeccability of Christ

	Peccability	Impeccability
Definition	Christ could sin.	Christ could not sin.
Key Phrase	Able not to sin (*Potuit non peccare*)	Not able to sin (*Non potuit peccare*)
Hebrews 4:15	Christ was tempted in all things as we are, yet he did not commit sin (sin is seen in its result). Real temptation admits the possibility of succumbing to the temptation.	Christ was tempted in all things as we are, but he did not have a sin nature (sin is seen as nature, or state of existence).
Question of True Humanity or True Deity	If Jesus could not sin, how could he be truly human?	If Jesus could sin, how could he be truly divine?
Points of Agreement	Christ's temptations were real (Heb. 4:15). Christ experienced struggle (Matt. 26:36-46). Christ did not sin (2 Cor. 5:21; Heb. 7:26; James 5:6; 1 Peter 2:22; 3:18; 1 John 3:5).	

	For Peccability	Against Peccability
Logical Argumentation for and Against Peccability	If Christ could be tempted, then he could have sinned. Peccability is a necessary deduction from temptability. Temptation implies the possibility of sin.	Temptability does not imply susceptibility. Just because an army can be attacked does not mean that it can be conquered. This also proceeds from the false assumption that what applies to us also applies necessarily to Christ.
	If Christ was not able to sin, then the temptation was not real and he cannot sympathize with his people.	Although Christ's temptations are not always exactly parallel to our own, he was tried through his human nature as we are. However, he had no sin nature and he was a divine person also.
	If Christ is impeccable, then his temptations were slight.	Christ's temptations were in every way like ours except that they did not originate in evil forbidden desires. He was tempted from without, not from within.
	If Christ could not sin, then he had no free will.	Christ manifested his free will by not sinning. Christ was free to do the will of the Father. Being of one will with the Father, he was not free to go against that will.

34. Theories of the Resurrection of Jesus Christ

I. Occupied Tomb Theories

Theory	Explanation	Refutation
Unknown Tomb Charles A. Guignebert	The body of Jesus was buried in a common pit grave unknown to his disciples. Therefore, the resurrection account arose out of the ignorance as to the whereabouts of the body.	Not all criminals were buried in a common pit. The New Testament gives Joseph of Arimathea as a witness to the burial in a specific family tomb. The women saw the body being prepared for burial and knew the tomb's location. The Romans knew where the tomb was, for they stationed a guard there.
Wrong Tomb Kirsopp Lake	The women came to the wrong tomb, for there were many similar tombs in Jerusalem. They found an open tomb and a young man who denied that this was Jesus' tomb. The frightened women mistakenly identified the man as an angel and fled.	The women did not come looking for an open tomb, but for a sealed one. They would surely bypass the open tomb if they were unsure of the exact location of the correct tomb. The man at the tomb not only said, "He is not here," but also "He is risen." The women had noted the tomb's location seventy-two hours earlier. The Jews, Romans, and Joseph of Arimathea knew the location of the tomb and could easily have identified it as proof against any resurrection.
Legend Early Form Critics	The resurrection was a fabrication that evolved over a lengthy period to vindicate a leader long since dead.	Recent historical criticism has shown that the resurrection stories are of mid–first-century origin. Paul, in 1 Corinthians (A.D. 55), speaks of the resurrection as a fact and points to five hundred eyewitnesses, many of whom were still alive for his readers to question.
Spiritual Resurrection Gnostics	Jesus' spirit was resurrected though his body was dead.	This denies a Jewish understanding of resurrection (bodily not spiritually). Christ ate and was touched and handled. The Jews could show the occupied tomb to their fellow Jews to prove the resurrection false.

Adapted from Josh McDowell, *Resurrection Factor* (San Bernardino: Here's Life, 1981). (Used by permission.

34. Theories of the Resurrection (continued)

Theory	Explanation	Refutation
Hallucination Agnostics	The disciples and followers of Jesus were so emotionally involved with Jesus' messianic expectation that their minds projected hallucinations of the risen Lord.	1. Over five hundred different people, in different situations, with differing degrees of commitment to Jesus, with different understandings of Jesus' teachings all had hallucinations? 2. Many appearances occurred to more than one person. Such simultaneous illusions are unlikely. 3. The disciples were not expecting Christ's resurrection. They viewed his death as final. 4. The Jews could have pointed to the occupied tomb to prove them false.

II. Unoccupied Tomb Theories

Theory	Explanation	Refutation
Passover Plot Hugh Schönfield	Jesus planned to fulfill the Old Testament prophecies of both suffering servant and ruling king through a mock death and resurrection. Joseph of Arimathea and a mysterious "young man" were co-conspirators. The plot went bad when the soldier speared Jesus, who later died. The "risen Lord" was the young man.	1. The guard posted at the tomb is ignored in Schönfield's theory. 2. The basis of the theory is faulty. The resurrection myths on which Jesus supposedly based his plot were not evident until the fourth century A.D. 3. Such a "resurrection" could not account for the dramatic change in the disciples. 4. All but four biblical witnesses are not accounted for, especially the five hundred eyewitnesses whom Paul spoke of as still living. 5. The whole plot of enduring crucifixion (and in doing so, alienating his national supporters) seems unlikely.
Resuscitation (Swoon) 18th–century Rationalists	Jesus did not die on the cross; he fainted from exhaustion. The cold temperature and spices revived him.	1. Medical science has proved that Jesus could not have survived the scourging and crucifixion. 2. Could this nearly dead Jesus make an impression as the risen Lord?

34. Theories of the Resurrection (continued)

Theory	Explanation	Refutation
Body Stolen by the Disciples Jews	The disciples stole the body while the guards were sleeping.	1. If the guards were sleeping, how did they know that the disciples stole the body? 2. Severe penalties, even death, would be the result of sleeping on duty. The highly disciplined guard would thus not have slept. 3. There is no way that the disciples could possibly overcome the guard. 4. It is preposterous to believe that the disciples died for a lie that they created.
Existential Resurrection Rudolf Bultmann	A historical resurrection will never be proved, but it is not necessary. The Christ of faith need not be bound to the historical Jesus. Rather, Christ is raised in our hearts.	The early disciples were convinced by historical events. They claimed to base their faith on what they saw, not on an existential need nor an a priori faith (Luke 24:33-35; 1 Cor. 15:3-8).
Historical Resurrection Orthodox Christianity	Jesus was resurrected by the power of God. He showed himself to his disciples and later ascended into heaven.	1. This view requires presuppositional changes, belief in God, supernaturalism. 2. This view virtually demands a faith in Jesus.

35. Biblical Teaching on the Holy Spirit

Category	Description/Definition	Scripture Reference
Names	Holy Spirit	Luke 11:13; John 20:22; Acts 1:5; cf. Ps. 51:11
	Spirit of Grace	Heb. 10:29
	Spirit of Truth	John 14:17; 15:26; 16:13; cf. 1 John 5:6
	Spirit of Wisdom and Knowledge	Isa. 11:2; cf. 61:1–2; 1 Tim. 1:17
	Spirit of Glory	1 Peter 4:14; cf. Exod. 15:11; Ps. 145:5
	Counselor	John 14:16; 16:7
Personality	He is the third person of the Godhead, the Trinity.	Matt. 3:16–17; John 14:16; Acts 10:38
	He has knowledge.	Isa. 11:2; Rom. 8:27; 1 Cor. 2;10–11
	He has feeling.	Isa. 63:10; Eph. 4:30; cf. Acts 7:51; Rom 15:30
	He has will.	1 Cor. 12:11
Attributes	He is divine.	Acts 5:3–4; 2 Cor. 3:18
	He is eternal.	Heb. 9:14
	He is omnipresent.	Ps. 139:7
	He is omniscient.	John. 14:26; 16:13; 1 Cor. 2:10
Works	He was active in creation.	Gen. 1:2; Job 33:4; Ps. 104:30
	He inspired the Bible writers.	2 Peter 1:21
	He empowered the conception of Christ.	Luke 1:35

35. Biblical Teaching on the Holy Spirit (continued)

Category	Description/Definition	Scripture Reference
Works (cont.)	He convicts of sin.	John 16:8; cf. Gen. 6:3
	He regenerates.	John 3:5–6
	He counsels.	John 14:16–17; 16:7,12–14
	He brings assurance of salvation.	Rom. 8:15
	He teaches or enlightens.	John 16:12–14; 1 Cor. 2:13
	He aids in prayer by intercession.	Rom. 8:26-27
	He resurrected Christ.	Rom. 8:11; 1 Peter 3:18
	He calls to service.	Acts 13:4
	He seals the elect's salvation.	Rom. 8:23; 2 Cor. 1:21-22; Eph. 1:13–14; 4:30
	He indwells the believer.	Rom. 8:9; 1 Cor. 3:16–17; 6:19
	He works in the church.	1 Cor. 12:7–11
Gifts	Source of all gifts to the church	1 Cor. 12:7–11
	Prophecy	1 Cor. 14:1–40
	Miracles and healing	1 Cor. 12:4, 28–30
	Tongues	1 Cor. 12:4,10
	Teaching	1 Cor. 12:4, 28
	Faith	1 Cor. 12:8–9
	Serving	1 Cor. 12:4, 28; Eph. 4:12
	Encouraging	Rom. 12:8; cf. 1 Cor. 12:4,7

36. Titles of the Holy Spirit

Title	Emphasis	Citation
One Spirit	His unity	Ephesians 4:4
Seven Spirits	His perfection, omnipresence, and completeness	Revelation 1:4; 3:1
The Lord the Spirit	His sovereignty	2 Corinthians 3:18
Eternal Spirit	His eternity	Hebrews 9:14
Spirit of Glory	His glory	1 Peter 4:14
Spirit of Life	His vitality	Romans 8:2
Spirit of Holiness Holy Spirit Holy One	His holiness	Romans 1:4 Matthew 1:20 1 John 2:20
Spirit of Wisdom Spirit of Understanding Spirit of Counsel Spirit of Knowledge	His omniscience, wisdom, and counsel	Isaiah 11:2 cf. 1 Cor. 2:10–13
Spirit of Might	His omnipotence	Isaiah 11:2
Spirit of Fear of the Lord	His reverence	Isaiah 11:2
Spirit of Truth	His truthfulness	John 14:17
Spirit of Grace	His grace	Hebrews 10:29
Spirit of Grace and Supplication	His grace and prayerfulness	Zechariah 12:10

Adapted from Paul Enns, *The Moody Handbook of Theology* (Chicago: Moody Press, 1989), p. 250. Used by permission.

37. The Work of the Holy Spirit in Salvation

Activity	Description of the Activity	Scripture Reference
Regeneration	Through the ministry of the Spirit a person is born again, receives eternal life, and is renewed.	John 3:3–8; 6:63; Titus 3:5
Indwelling	The Spirit abides in the believer. Without the Spirit's indwelling the person does not belong to Christ.	John 14:17; Romans 8:9,11; 1 Corinthians 3:16; 6:19
Baptizing	Believers are baptized in the Holy Spirit by Christ, uniting them all into one body.	Matthew 3:11; Mark 1:8; Luke 3:16; 1 Corinthians 12:13
Sealing	God seals believers with the Holy Spirit, providing a statement of ownership and guarantee of final redemption.	2 Corinthians 1:22; Ephesians 1:13; 4:30; cf. Romans 8:16
Filling	Believers are commanded to be "filled with the Spirit." The filling ministry of the Spirit can be divided into the general filling relating to spiritual growth and maturation and to special capacities given by the Spirit for special tasks for God.	Ephesians 5:18; cf. Acts 4:8; 4:31; 6:3; 9:17; 11:24; 13:9
Guiding	Believers are commanded to walk in the Spirit and be led by the Spirit. The Spirit keeps the believer from enslavement to legalism and also provides discipline and direction for the Christian life.	Galatians 5:16, 25; cf. Acts 8:29; 13:2; 15:7–9; 16:6; Romans 8:14
Empowering	The indwelling Spirit provides victory in the Christian life, development of Christian fruit, and the ability to win against the works of Satan.	Romans 8:13; Galatians 5:17–18, 22–23
Teaching	Jesus promised that when the Spirit came he would lead believers into truth. The Spirit illuminates the mind of the believer to the revelation of God's will through his Word.	John 14:26; 16:13; 1 John 2:20, 27

38. Four Groupings of Spiritual Gifts

1 Corinthians 12:8-10	1 Corinthians 12:29-30	Romans 12:6-8	Ephesians 4:11
Word of Wisdom			
Word of Knowledge			
Gifts of Healing	Gifts of Healing		
Miracles	Miracles		
Prophecy	Prophecy	Prophecy	Prophecy
Discerning of Spirits	Discerning of Spirits		
Tongues	Tongues		
Interpretation of Tongues			
	Apostles		Apostles
	Teachers	Teaching	Teaching [or Teaching Pastors]
	Helps		
		Ministry	
		Encouraging	
		Giving	
		Leadership	
		Showing Mercy	
	Administration		
			Evangelists
			Pastors

39. Summary of Spiritual Gifts

Gift	Description	Result	Example
Prophecy προφητεια Rom. 12:6 1 Cor. 14:29–32	Speaking truth directly revealed from God	Understanding mystery 1 Cor. 13:2	Timothy—1 Tim. 4:14 Daughters of Philip—Acts 21:8–9
Service, Helping διακονια Rom. 12:7	Aiding others to do God's work Giving practical assistance to members of the church	Serving the church and the needy Acts 6:1	Onesiphorus 2 Tim. 1:16
Teaching διδασκαλια Rom. 12:7 1 Cor. 12:28 Eph. 4:11	Communicating the truth and applications of the Scripture	Understanding the Word of God Acts 18:26	Priscilla and Aquila—Acts 18:26 Apollos—Acts 18:27–28 Paul—Acts 18:11
Encouraging παρακλησις Rom. 12:8	Urging one to pursue proper conduct or to console	Encouragement Acts 9:27	Barnabas Acts 4:36
Giving μεταδιδωμι Rom. 12:8	Liberally and cheerfully imparting substance to God's work	Meeting physical needs Acts 9:36	Dorcas Acts 9:36
Leadership προιστημι Rom. 12:8	Organizing and administering the work of the ministry	Order Titus 1:5	Titus Titus 1:5

39. Summary of Spiritual Gifts (continued)

Gift	Description	Result	Example
Showing Mercy ελεεω Rom. 12:8	Giving undeserved aid to others	Sympathy, compassion toward undeserving	Barnabas Acts 9:27
Apostleship αποστολος 1 Cor. 12:28 Eph. 4:11	Being an eyewitness of the resurrected Christ and speaking authoritatively about faith and practice	Sets forth God's precepts for the church 1 Cor. 14:37	Paul—Gal. 1:1 Peter—1 Peter 1:1
Evangelism ευαγγελιστης Eph. 4:11	Presenting the gospel with clarity and with a burden for the unsaved	Understanding the Gospel	Philip Acts 21:8
Pastor/Teacher ποιμην Rom 12:7; Eph. 4:11	Shepherding and teaching the church	Care and godly instruction Acts 20:28–31	Paul 1 Thess. 2:7–12
The Message of Wisdom λογος σοφιας 1Cor. 12:8	Perceiving and presenting the truth of God Applying God's Word or wisdom to specific situations	The ability to grasp and apply the revelation given	John 1 John 1:1–3
The Message of Knowledge λογος γνωσεως 1 Cor. 12:8	Understanding and exhibiting wisdom from God Revelation from God about people, circumstances, or biblical truth	Truth understood in its spiritual sense 1 Cor. 2:6–12	Paul Col. 2:2–3

39. Summary of Spiritual Gifts (continued)

Gift	Description	Result	Example
Faith πιστις 1 Cor. 12:9	Trusting God implicitly to perform unusual deeds	Accomplishment of great tasks	Stephen Acts 6:5
Healing ιαμα 1 Cor. 12:9	Being able to cure diseases	Complete cures Acts 3:6–7	Peter and John—Acts 3:6–7 Paul—Acts 20:9-12
Miracles δυναμις 1 Cor. 12:10	Being able to perform works of power	People fear God Acts 5:9–11	Paul Acts 13:8–11
Discernment διακρισις 1 Cor. 12:10	Distinguishing the power by which a teacher or prophet speaks	Exposure of false prophets 1 John 4:1	Believers at Corinth 1 Cor. 14:29
Tongues γλωσσα 1 Cor. 12:10	Speaking in a language not understood by the speaker	Praise to God which is understood by those persons knowing the language spoken (Acts 2:1-12) Thanksgiving to God which may be understood if someone interprets the language spoken (1 Cor. 14:5, 16, 27-28)	The disciples
Interpretation ερμηνεια 1 Cor. 12:10	Making "tongues" understandable	Confirmation of the foreign language 1 Cor. 14:27–28	

40. Viewpoints on "Tongues"

Category	Traditional	Pentecostal	Charismatic
Nature of Tongues	Tongues in Acts are human languages whereas tongues in 1 Corinthians are either human languages, heavenly or angelic languages, or ecstatic utterances.	Tongues in Acts are human languages whereas tongues in 1 Corinthians are heavenly or angelic languages.	Tongues in Acts are human languages whereas tongues in 1 Corinthians are heavenly or angelic languages.
Content of Tongues	Glossolalia is praying to God in a language that one has not studied. Some believe that New Testament accounts of "tongues" ties it in with a knowable or known language which is addressed to God in thanksgiving and praise. Never is it intended that tongues be equivalent to prophecy in being addressed to people.	Tongues may be prayer to God or they may be God's means of speaking to the people of God, equivalent to prophecy, if interpreted.	Tongues may be prayer to God or they may be God's means of speaking to the people of God, equivalent to prophecy, if interpreted.
Need of Tongues	Dispensationalists believe that tongues had a limited value in the early church to demonstrate God's change from Israel to the church. Most are in agreement that they were also used to build up the church when accompanied by the gift of interpretation of tongues. They are not needed today.	Tongues not only to signify the Spirit's presence and power but also to provide the ability to speak to God through the Spirit about concerns that the mind is not able to express. The gift of tongues is also given to some Christians to give the will of God.	Not all Christians will speak in tongues, and the Spirit is present in every Christian, but special power comes to the Christian by means of releasing the Spirit's power by tongues, given to some Christians to give the will of God to the church for its edification.
Purpose of Tongues	The primary purpose of tongues was to demonstrate the change from the nation of Israel to the nations of all the world. They are not a normative indication that someone has received the Spirit of God or a second baptism of (or in) the Spirit.	Tongues are the initial, necessary evidence that one has received the Spirit or the empowering from the Spirit by means of the baptism of the Holy Spirit. Further, they are used by the Spirit-filled believer in praying more effectively. Pentecostals differ as to whether one receives the Spirit of God at the moment of conversion or only at the baptism of the Spirit.	Tongues are an indicator (but not the only one) that one has the fullness of the Spirit of God. All Christians have the Spirit from conversion, but the fullness comes through one's letting God take control of one's life. This is not a second blessing but a recognition of God's power. Tongues help one to pray in the Spirit.
Duration of Tongues	Tongues ceased after the completion of the New Testament. There is no reliable evidence today of the miraculous gift of speaking foreign languages.	Tongues have continued throughout the ages, arising again in various periods of the church's history when greater desire for spirituality has occurred.	Tongues have continued throughout the ages, arising again in various periods of the church's history when greater desire for spirituality occurred.

41. A Comparison of Angels, Humans, and Animals

Category	Angels	Humans	Animals
Image of God	No	Yes	No
Nature/Existence			
Body	Immaterial/spirit	Immaterial/physical	Material/physical
	Influence through humans	Influence by spirits	
	No marriage or propagation	Marriage/propagation	No marriage, but propagation
Personality	Full personality	Full personality	Partial personality
	Emphasis on will/obedience	Emphasis on will/obedience	Emphasis on subordination
Sin	Prideful rebellion: desire to be "like God"	Prideful rebellion: desire to be "like God"	Nonmoral, derived from man or Satan (Gen. 3)
Relation to God	Direct	Direct	Indirect
	Heavenly/earthly	Earthly/heavenly	Earthly under man
Function/Purpose	Influence on earth under God	Dominion on earth under God	Service on earth under man

Adapted from chart by Lanier Burns. Used by permission.

42. Sons of God in Genesis Six

Position	Angelic Creatures	Apostate Sethites	Ambitious Despots
Persons	Fallen angels cohabit with beautiful women	Ungodly Sethites marry depraved Cainites	Despotic chieftains marry plurality of wives
Perversion	Perversion of human race by intrusion of angels	Pollution of godly line by mixed marriage	Polygamy of Cainite princes to expand dominion
Progeny	Monstrous giants	Wicked tyrants	Dynastic rulers
Proofs	The reference to angels as "sons of God"	The emphasis on men in the context	The antiquity of this interpretation
	The New Testament references to the angelic sin of Genesis 6 in 2 Peter 2:4–5 and Jude 6–7	The basis for human sin as the reason for the Flood	The biblical usage of "god" for rulers and judges
	The antiquity of the view	The thematic development of Genesis 4 and 5	The reference in the context to the development of wicked dynasties
	The satisfactory explanation that some angels are bound and others are not	The aversion in Genesis and elsewhere to intermarriage between the godly and ungodly	The Near Eastern practice of calling kings "sons of God"
			The reference in ancient accounts to the origin of kingship just prior to the Flood
Problems	The psychological and physiological impossibilities of angelic marriages	The textual difficulty in making "men" of Genesis 6:1 different from "men" in verse 2	The lack of evidence that such a system was established in the line of Cain
	The likelihood that "sons of God" refers to men, since it is used elsewhere of men	The absence of exact terms "sons of God" for believers in the Old Testament	The lack of evidence that "sons of God" was borrowed from contemporary literature
		Failure to explain the origin of the giants and mighty men through simply religiously mixed marriages	The fact that no writer of Scripture ever considered kings to be deities
Proponents	Albright, Gaebelein, Kelly, Unger, Waltke, Delitzsch, Bullinger, Larkin, Pember, Wuest, Gray, Torrey, Meyer, Mayor, Plummer, Alford, Ryrie, Smith	Hengstenberg, Keil, Lange, Jamieson, Fausset, Brown, Henry, Scofield, Lincoln, Murray, Baxter, Scroggie, Leupold	Kaiser, Birney, Kline, Cornfeld, Kober

43. Biblical Teaching on Angels

	Unfallen	Fallen
Origin	Angels were created as holy beings (Mark 8:38) by God (Col. 1:16) before the creation of the earth (Job 38:7) by fiat (Ps. 148:2, 5).	
Nature	Angels were created with the ability to fellowship and with personality expressed by intellect (1 Peter 1:12), emotion (Job 38:7), and will (Isa. 14:12-15), but they are never said to be in the image of God, as man is. They are localized beings (Dan. 9:21-23), immortal (Luke 20:36), and have limited knowledge (Matt. 24:36). They are normally invisible (Col. 1:16) but have appeared to people in the form of male beings (Gen. 18:1-8), sometimes very unusual men (Dan. 10:5-6), and at times with some sort of supernatural dazzle (Matt. 28:3) and as unusual living creatures in heaven (Rev. 4:6-8). Usually their appearance affects the human concerned to respond in fear and agitation (Luke 1:29).	
Spiritual Condition	Although all angels were created good, there are now two moral classifications: holy and elect (Mark 8:38; 1 Tim. 5:21) and evil and unclean (Luke 8:2; 11:24-26). They are aligned either with God (John 1:51) or with Satan (Matt. 25:41).	
Similarities With Man	Created by God, localized, accountable to God (John 16:11), limited in knowledge (Matt. 24:36).	
Differences From Man	Different order of being (Heb. 2:5-7), invisible, do not procreate (Matt. 22:28-30), greater in intelligence, strength, and swiftness (2 Peter 2:11), not subject to physical death.	
Classifications	Rulers, powers, world forces (Eph. 6:12), dominion (Eph. 1:21) thrones (Col. 1:16).	
Purpose	To serve God in worship (Rev. 4:6-11), in ministry (Heb. 1:7), in being God's messengers (Ps. 103:20), to act in God's government (Dan. 10:13, 21), protecting God's people (Ps. 34:7), executing God's judgment (Gen. 19:1).	To promote Satan's program in opposing God (Rev. 12:7) by promoting rebellion (Gen. 3), idolatry (Lev. 17:7), false religions (1 John 4:1-4), and oppression of mankind.
Relationship to Believers	Reveal truth (Gal. 3:19), guide (Mt. 1:20-21); provide physical needs (1 Kings 19:6), protect (Dan. 3:24-28), deliver (Acts 5:17-20), encourage (Acts 5:19-20), act in answering prayer (Dan. 9:20-24), accompany the dead (Luke 16:22).	Wage war (Eph. 6:10-18), accuse (Rev. 12:10), plant doubt (Gen. 3:1-3), tempt to sin (Eph. 2:1-3), persecute (Rev. 12:1-3), prevent service (1 Thess. 2:18), disturb the church (2 Cor. 2:10-11).
Relationship to Christ on Earth	Announced the birth of Christ (Luke 1:26-38), guided Joseph to safety (Matt. 2:14), ministered to Christ (Matt. 4:11; Luke 22:43), announced his resurrection (Matt. 28:2-4), ascension and return (Acts 1:11).	Satan tempted Christ (Mark 1:13), led people to betray and kill Him (Luke 22:3-4); Christ cast demons out and finally defeated them on the cross (Col. 2:15).
Place of Habitation	In God's presence (Isa. 6:1-6), heavenly realms (Eph. 3:10)	Heavenly (spiritual) realms (Eph. 6:12), abyss (Rev. 9:1-11), people (Mark 9:14-29), the bonds of darkness (Jude 6).
Destiny	To be in God's presence and Christ's presence in his kingdom (Rev. 21-22)	Defeated by Christ (Col. 2:15), cast into the abyss during Millennium (Rev. 20:1-2), cast into lake of fire as final punishment (Rev. 20:10).
Specific Angels	Michael, Gabriel	Satan

44. The Doctrine of Satan and Demons

	Satan
	Heb. *sätän*, Gr. *satanas*, an adversary, opponent
	(1 Chron. 21:1; Job 1:6; John 13:27; Acts 5:3; 26:18; Rom. 16:20)

Names and Titles	Scripture	Doctrine of Satan Categorized
Abaddon	Rev. 9:11	**Description** — Subtle (Gen. 3:1), provoker (1 Chron. 21:1), owner of the kingdoms and glory of the world (Matt. 4:8), murderer and without truth (John 8:44), full of subtlety, all mischief, enemy of all righteousness, perverter of the right ways of the Lord (Acts 13:10). Has power, signs, and lying wonders (2 Thess. 2:9). Sinner from the beginning (1 John 3:8), deceiver of the whole world (Rev. 12:9). Can appear as an angel of light (2 Cor. 11:14). Leads his followers (1 Tim. 5:15). His children called tares (Matt. 13:38).
Accuser of our brothers	Rev. 12:10	
Adversary	1 Peter 5:8	
Angel of the Abyss	Rev. 9:11	
Apollyon	Rev. 9:11	
Beelzebub	Matt. 12:24; Mark 3:22; Luke 11:15	
Belial	2 Cor. 6:15	**Activities/Works** — **General Description.** Provokes (1 Chron. 21:1), goes to and fro on the earth (Job 1:7), can cause physical illness (Job 2:7), can blind people (Luke 13:16), spiritually blinds unbelievers (2 Cor .4:4), shoots flaming arrows (Eph. 6:16), hinders (1 Thess. 2:18), condemns and snares (1 Tim. 3:16), seeks to devour (1 Peter 5:8), takes away sown Word of God (Matt. 13:19), wants to take advantage (2 Cor. 2:11), transforms into an angel of light (2 Cor. 11:14). **Specific Examples:** Bruised Christ's heel (Gen. 3:15), tempted Jesus (Matt 4:1), desired to sift Simon Peter as wheat (Luke 22:31), entered into and persuaded Judas to betray Jesus (John 13:2, 27), filled the heart of Ananias to lie (Acts 5:3), will cast some into prison (Rev. 2:10).
The devil	Matt. 4:1; Luke 4:2; Rev. 20:2	
Enemy	Matt. 13:39	
Evil spirit	1 Sam. 16:14	
Father of lies	John 8:44	
Great red dragon	Rev. 12:3	
Liar	John 8:44	
Lying spirit	1 Kings 22:22	
Murderer	John 8:44	
Ancient serpent	Rev. 12:9; 20:2	**Limitations** — Must receive permission from God (Job 1:12), head crushed by Christ, Christ's heel bruised by Satan (Gen. 3:15), can be resisted (James 4:7), can be overcome (1 John 2:13), overcome by the blood of the Lamb (Rev. 12:11), cannot touch those begotten of God (1 John 5:18).
Power of darkness	Col. 1:13	
Prince of this world	John 12:31	
Prince of devils	Matt.12:24	
Ruler of the kingdom of the air	Eph. 2:2	
Power of this dark world	Eph. 6:12	**Destiny** — Head crushed by Christ (Gen. 3:15), will be crushed by the God of peace (Rom. 16:20), his power of death destroyed by Jesus (Heb. 2:14), works destroyed by the Son of God (1 John 3:8), bound for 1,000 years (Rev. 20:1), cast into the bottomless pit (Rev. 20:3), loosed after 1,000 years to deceive the nations (Rev. 20:8), cast into the lake of fire (Rev. 20:10), rebuked by the Lord (Zech. 3:2), doomed to everlasting fire (Matt. 25:41), cast from heaven (Luke 10:18), judged by God (John 16:11).
Serpent	Gen. 3:4, 14; 2 Cor. 1:3	
Spirit at work in those who are disobedient	Eph. 2:2	
Tempter	Matt. 4:3; 1 Thess. 3:5	
The god of this world	2 Cor. 4:4	
Unclean spirit	Matt. 12:43	
Evil one	Matt. 13:19, 38	

44. Doctrine of Satan and Demons (continued)

Demons Gr. *daimon*, *daimonion*, fallen spirits		
Occurrences in Scripture	**Scripture**	**Doctrine of Demons Categorized**
Worship of demons forbidden	Lev. 17:7; Deut. 32:17; 2 Chron. 11:15; Ps. 106:37; Zech. 13:2; Matt. 4:9; Luke 4:7; Rev. 9:20; 13:4	**Description** Angels who fell with Satan (Matt. 12:24), divided into two groups: one group is active in opposing God's people Rev. 9:14; 16:14) and another is confined in prison (2 Peter 2:4; Jude 6), intelligent (Mark 1:24), know their doom (Matt. 8:29), know the plan of salvation (James 2:19), have their own doctrine (1 Tim. 4:1-3).
Possession by, instances of	1 Sam. 16:14-23; 18:10–11; 19:9, 10	
Two men of the Gergesenes	Matt. 8:28–34; Mark 5:2–20	
The dumb man	Matt. 9:32–33	
The blind and dumb man	Matt. 12:22; Luke 11:14	**Activities/Works** Seek to hinder the plan of God (Dan. 10:10-14; Rev 16:13-16), inflict illnesses (Matt. 9:33; Luke 13:11-16), possess animals (Mark 5:13), promote false doctrine (1 Tim. 4:1), influence nations (Isa. 14; Ezek. 28; Dan. 10:13; Rev. 16:13-14), possess unbelievers (Matt. 9:32-33;10:18; Mark 6:13).
The daughter of the Syrian Phoenician	Matt. 15:22–29; Mark 7:25–30; Luke 9:37–42	
The lunatic child	Matt. 17:14–18; Mark 9:17–27	
The man in the syna-gogue	Mark 1:23–26; Luke 4:33–35	
The herd of swine cast out by Jesus	Matt. 4:24; 8:16, 30–32; Mark 3:22; Luke 4:41	
Power over, given the disciples	Matt. 10:1; Mark 6:7; 16:17	
Cast out by the disciples	Mark 9:38; Acts 5:16; Acts 8:7;16:16-18; 19:12	**Limitations** Limited in space like unfallen angels (Matt. 17:18; Mark 9:25), are used by God for his purposes when he desires (1 Sam. 16:14; 2 Cor. 12:7), may be cast out and return to former person from whom cast out (Luke 11:24-26).
Disciples unable to expel	Mark 9:18, 28–29	
Sceva's sons exorcise	Acts 19:13–16	
Parable of the man repossessed	Matt. 12:43–45	
Jesus falsely accused of having	Mark 3:22-30; John 7:20; 8:48; 10:20	**Destiny** Some free in the time of Christ have been cast into the abyss (Luke 8:31), some now confined will be loosed during tribulation (Rev. 9:1-11; 16:13-14), will be cast along with Satan into lake of fire forever (Matt. 25:41).
Testify to deity of Jesus	Matt. 8:29; Mark 1:23, 24; 3:11; 5:7; Luke 8:28; Acts 19:15	
Adversaries of people	Matt. 12:45	
Sent to cause trouble between Abimelech and the Shechemites	Judges 9:23	
Gave messages to false prophets	1 Kings 22:21–23	
Believe and tremble	James 2:19	
To be judged	Matt. 8:29; 2 Peter 2:4; Jude 6	
Punishment of	Matt. 8:29; 25:41; Luke 8:28; 2 Peter 2:4; Jude 6; Rev. 12:7-9	
Possession (Mary Magdalene)	Mark 16:9; Luke 8:2, 3	

45. Names of Satan

Title	Emphasis	Citation
Satan	Adversary	Matthew 4:10
Devil	Slanderer	Matthew 4:1
Evil One	Intrinsically evil	John 17:15
Great red dragon	Destructive creature	Revelation 12:3,7,9
Serpent of old	Deceiver in Eden	Revelation 12:9
Abaddon	Destruction	Revelation 9:11
Apollyon	Destroyer	Revelation 9:11
Adversary	Opponent	1 Peter 5:8
Beelzebub	Lord of the fly (Baalzebub)	Matthew 12:24
Belial	Worthless (Beliar)	2 Corinthians 6:15
God of this world	Controls philosophy of this world	2 Corinthians 4:4
Ruler of this world	Rules in world system	John 12:31
Prince of the power of the air	Control of believers	Ephesians 2:2
Enemy	Opponent	Matthew 13:28; 1 Peter 5:8
Tempter	Solicits people to sin	Matthew 4:3
Murderer	Leads people to eternal death	John 8:44
Liar	Perverts the truth	John 8:44
Accuser	Opposes believers before God	Revelation 12:10

Adapted from Paul Enns, *The Moody Handbook of Theology* (Chicago: Moody Press, 1989), p. 293. Used by permission.

46. Theories Concerning the Constitution of Man

Dichotomy	
Man as a Twofold Being	
Arguments for	**Arguments Against**
God breathed into man but one principle–a living soul (Gen. 2:7).	The Hebrew text is plural, "Then the Lord God formed man of dust from the ground and breathed into his nostrils the breath of life (lives); and man became a living being."
The immaterial part of man (the soul) is viewed as an individual and conscious life, capable of possessing and animating a physical organism (body).	Paul states that man has both a spirit and a soul, which are housed in a physical body (1 Thess. 5:23).
The terms "soul" and "spirit" seem to be used interchangeably in some references (Gen. 41:8 and Ps. 42:6; Matt. 20:28 and 27:50; Jn. 12:27 and 13:21; Heb. 12:23 and Rev. 6:9).	Hebrews 4:12 speaks of the separation of the soul from the spirit. If they were the same, they could not be divided.
"Spirit" (as well as "soul") is ascribed to brute creation (Eccl. 3:21; Rev. 16:3).	The term "spirit" or "soul" may be used for animal "life" or "animation" but never in the unique sense in which human spirit or soul is used. Human spirits continue beyond physical existence, unlike the animals, and human spirits are in relationship with the divine spirit of God (Matt. 17:3; Acts 7:59; Gal. 6:8; 1 Thess. 5:23; Rev. 16:3).
Body and soul are spoken of as constituting the whole person (Matt. 10:28; 1 Cor. 5:3; 3 John 2).	The spirit, soul, and body are spoken of as constituting the whole person (Mark 12:30; 1 Cor. 2:14; 3:4; 1 Thess. 5:23).
Consciousness testifies that there are two elements in man's being. We can distinguish a material part and an immaterial part, but the consciousness of no one can distinguish between soul and spirit.	It is the spirit of man that deals with the spiritual realm. The soul is the dimension of man that deals with the mental realm, man's intellect, the sensibilities, and the will–the part that reasons and thinks. The body is the part of man that contacts or deals with the physical realm. Hebrews 4:12 does literally speak of the separation of the soul from the spirit (1 Thess. 5:23; cf. John 3:7; Rom. 2:28-29; 1 Cor. 2:14; 14:14).

46. Constitution of Man (continued)

Trichotomy
Man as a Threefold Being

Arguments for	Arguments Against
Genesis 2:7 does not absolutely declare that God made a twofold being. The Hebrew text is plural, "The Lord God formed man from the dust of the ground and breathed into his nostrils the breath of life [lives], and man became a living being."	It is not said that man became spirit and soul. And further, "living being" is the same phrase used of animals and translated "living creature" (Gen. 1:21–24).
Paul seems to think of the body, soul, and spirit as three distinct parts of man's nature (1 Thess. 5:23). The same seems to be indicated in Hebrews 4:12, where the Word is said to pierce "even to dividing soul and spirit, joints and marrow."	Paul is emphasizing the whole person, not attempting to differentiate his parts. Hebrews 4:12 does not speak of the separation of the soul from the spirit, but of the separation itself extending to that point. The Word pierces to the dividing of the soul itself and spirit itself. The soul and spirit are laid open.
A threefold organization of man's nature may be implied in the classification of man as "natural," "carnal," and "spiritual," in 1 Corinthians 2:14; 3:1–4 (KJV).	Body and soul are spoken of as constituting the whole person (Matt. 10:28; 1 Cor. 5:3; 3 John 2).
In Luke 8:55, we read about the girl whom Jesus raised from the dead that "her spirit [*pneuma*] returned." And so when Christ died, it is said that "he gave up his life," "he dismissed his spirit," (Matt. 27:50). "The body without the spirit is dead" (James 2:27). *Pneuma* refers to a life principle apart from the soul.	*Pneuma* (spirit) and *psyche* (soul) are used interchangeably throughout the New Testament. Both represent one life principle.

47. The Dimensions of the *Imago Dei*

	The image of God in man has been marred but not erased (Gen. 9:6; 1 Cor. 11:7; James 3:9).
Rational Dimension	Man was given responsibility to exercise dominion over the earth (Gen. 1:26–28; Ps. 8:4–9). Adam was commanded to take care of the garden. Adam named the animals (Gen. 19–20). Adam recognized that the woman was a helper suitable for him (Gen. 2:22–24; cf. 2:20).
Spiritual Dimension	Adam and Eve had fellowship with God (Gen. 3:8). Adam and Eve feared God after their sin (Gen. 3:10).
Moral Dimension	God gave Adam and Eve a moral command (Gen. 2:17). Adam and Eve had a sense of moral rectitude (Gen. 2:25). Adam and Eve experienced guilt following their transgression (Gen. 3:7). This seems to indicate that the image included original righteousness (Gen. 1:31; Eccles. 7:29).
Social Dimension	Adam and Eve conversed with each other [presumably] (Gen. 2:18, 23; 3:6–8; 4:1).

48. Views on the Nature of the *Imago Dei*

Viewpoint	Support	Problems
Substantive View The image of God consists in a definite physical, psychological, and/or spiritual characteristic within the nature of man.	Image (*tselem*) in Genesis 1:26 can be translated "statue;" hence, the passage may read, "Let us make man to look like us." In John 1:14–18 (and elsewhere) it is made clear that Jesus was God and that he had a human body.	This view defines God by defining man. God is spirit (see John 4:24). In what way, then, does our physical body represent God? Also, birds and other animals have bodies and are not said to have been made in the image of God (see Gen. 1:20–23).
Functional View The image of God consists in what man does.	Genesis 1:26–28 clearly says that man is to rule or have dominion over the rest of creation. God clearly rules.	Genesis 1:27 indicates that God created man in his image before he gave man dominion. Therefore the *Imago Dei* may be other than the capacity for dominion.
Relational View Only when we have faith in (i.e., "interact with") Jesus Christ do we fully possess the image of God.	God created "man" male and female (Gen. 1:26–27), indicating the relational aspect of God in humankind. Also Exodus 20; Mark 12:28–31; Luke 10:26–27 suggest the relational dimensions of God and humankind. The entire Word of God records God's relational nature.	Genesis 9:6 and James 3:9 make it clear that unregenerate man has also been created in the image of God.
Reformed View The image of God in man is man's conscious propensities and man's true knowledge. Part of the image of God in man (i.e., his "natural image") is obscured, but not destroyed by sin; and part of God's "moral image" is lost to man as the result of sin but is restored by Christ.	Part of the image of God in man is man's spiritual, moral, and immortal being, which has been "defaced but not erased." (See Gen. 8:15–9:7; Ps. 8:4–9; 1 Cor. 11:7; 15:49; Heb. 2:5–8.) Man's knowledge of righteousness and holiness is lost because of sin and restored by Christ. (See Eph. 4:22–25; Col. 3:9–10.) God is conscious and possesses true knowledge.	Genesis 1:26–28 does not refer to divisions of the image of God; rather it speaks of a single image of God.

49. Theories of Original Righteousness

Viewpoint	Viewpoint
Pelagian	There is free will; there is no such thing as original righteousness. "Man was endowed with reason, so that he could know God; with free will, so that he was able to choose and do the good; and with the necessary power to rule the lower creation." "All good and evil, by which we are praised or blameworthy, does not originate together with us, but is done by us. We are born capable of each, but not filled with either. And so we are produced without virtue, so are we also without vice; and before the action of his own will, there is in man only what God made."
Thomas Aquinas	Righteousness is a gift added after man's creation. Primitive holiness was purely a supernatural endowment or gift. As such it must be extraneous to the nature of Adam and conferred subsequently to his completed creation. "God formed man out of the clay . . . But as to his soul, he formed him after his own image and likeness. . . . Then he added the admirable gift of original righteousness. . . ."
Augustinian	Righteousness is part of the original human nature. It was an intrinsic quality of the nature of man. By the divine creative act man was constituted holy, and there was not only no subsequent act, but also no separate act by which he was so constituted. That nature was so constituted as to be responsive to the claims of a prudent and good life, not in the sense of a necessary fulfillment of such claims, but in the sense of a spontaneous inclination or disposition toward such fulfillment.

50. Theories of Original Sin

Viewpoint	Argument
Pelagianism	Man's soul is created by God (each individual near or at birth).
	Man's soul is created without corruption.
	The influence of Adam's sin is that of an example.
	Man has free volition.
	God's grace is universal since all men have free will; adults may obtain forgiveness through baptism.
	Thus, Adam's sin does not directly affect others, there is no such thing as original sin, and man is not depraved.
	Since man is not born in sin, it is possible for him to be preserved and to never need salvation.
Arminianism	Man receives from Adam a corrupted nature but does not receive Adam's guilt.
	This nature is corrupted physically and intellectually, but not volitionally.
	Prevenient grace enables man to believe.
	Thus, man is not totally depraved, but still retains the volition to seek God.
Calvinism	Each individual is related to Adam. There are two primary views:
	Federal Headship (creationist view of origin of the soul)
	The individual receives the physical nature from parents.
	God creates each soul.
	Adam was our representative, as ordained by God.
	This representation parallels man's being in Christ unto righteousness
	Natural Headship (traducianist view of origin of soul—Augustine)
	The individual receives the physical nature and the soul from the parents.
	Thus, all people were present in Adam in germinal or seminal form.
	Each individual participates in the sin of Adam.
	Thus, each individual inherits Adam's sin.

51. The Imputation of Adam's Sin

Key passage: Romans 5:12-21/Key Phrase: ἐφ' ᾧ πάντες ἥμαρτον (12d)

Distinguishing the Views

The Example View

Adam's sin was a minor act of disobedience that affected only himself. Romans 5:12d refers to the actual personal sins of individuals who followed Adam's example, committed sins, and are thus guilty before God.

The Solidarity View

A solidarity exists between Adam and his race such that Paul can say that one sinned (cf. 5:13-19) and at the same time say that all sinned (cf. 5:12). Both statements refer to the Fall.

Seminalism

The union between Adam and his posterity is biological and genetic such that Adam embodied all human beings in a single collective entity and thus all people are co-sinners with Adam.

Federalism

The union between Adam and his posterity is due to the fact that God appointed him as the representative head of the human race. What Adam did is charged to his posterity.

Mediate (Indirect) Imputation

People have a corrupt nature imputed to them--the effect of Adam's sin. Thus hereditary depravity is imputed. All sinned because all have inherited natural corruption from Adam.

Immediate (Direct) Imputation

Adam's first sin was imputed to every person. All people were tried in Adam our representative and declared guilty.

51. The Imputation of Adam's Sin (continued)

Understanding the Views

Viewpoint	What is a person's condition in relation to God at birth?	What are the effects of Adam's sin on his posterity?	How did all sin?	What is imputed (charged to one's account)?
Pelagianism*	He is innocent and able to obey God.	It had no effect. Adam's sin affected only himself.	All chose to sin by following Adam's example.	Only an individual's personal sins
Arminianism*	He has a sinful nature but is still able to cooperate with the Spirit by prevenient grace.	It corrupted them physically and intellectually, but the guilt of Adam's sin was not imputed to them.	All consciously ratify Adam's deed by personal sins. Mediate cause: All sin because they possess a corrupt nature inherited from Adam.	Only an individual's personal sins
Realism	His entire nature is polluted by sin; he is under condemnation and unable to merit saving favor with God.	It brought personal guilt, corruption, and death to all.	All participate in the sin of Adam, who is the natural head of the race.	Adam's sin, guilt, a corrupt nature, and one's own sins (Realism and Federalism differ only in the manner of imputation.)
Federalism	His entire nature is polluted by sin; he is under condemnation and unable to merit saving favor with God.	It brought condemnation and pollution by sin to the entire nature of all.	Mediate cause: All sin because they possess a corrupt nature inherited from Adam. Immediate cause: All sin because all are constituted sinners on account of Adam's sin.	Mediate imputation: A corrupt nature and one's own sins. Immediate imputation: Adam's sin guilt, a corrupt nature, and one's own sins.

*Pelagianism and Arminianism subscribe in differing measure to the view that people sin by following the example of Adam.

51. The Imputation of Adam's Sin (continued)

Evaluating the Views

Viewpoint	Translation of ἐφ᾽ ᾧ in Romans 5:12	Critique
The Example View	"that is why"	The aorist tense of ἥμαρτον suggests all sinned in or with Adam, not subsequent to Adam. In 5:15-19 it is stated five times that only one sin caused the death of all. The example view ignores the analogy between Adam and Christ.
Seminalism	"in whom" (i.e., in Adam)	Hebrews 7:9-10 provides an example of one man (Abraham) including another (Levi). Seminalism weakens the analogy between Adam and Christ, posits an unattested denotation of ἐφ᾽ ᾧ in the Pauline Corpus and begs certain absurd questions (e.g. Can someone act before he "exists"? Why are we not responsible for Adam's later sins?).
Mediate Imputation View	"because"	ἐφ᾽ ᾧ means "because" in 2 Corinthians 5:4 (cf. Phil. 3:12; 4:10). Mediate imputation faces certain contextual difficulties in Rom. 5: (1) ἁμαρτανω does not mean "to have a corrupt nature"; (2) both Adam and his posterity die from Adam's one trespass (vv. 12, 18-19) and no intermediate condition is cited; (3) γάρ (5:13-14) introduces an explanation that is not consistent with the argument of 5:12 if this view is adopted.
Immediate Federalism	"because"	Immediate Federalism faces the problem of explaining how the sin of one man, Adam, can be counted against the entire human race. Deuteronomy 24:16 says that "each is to die for his own sin," which appears contradictory to the Federalist view. Moreover, alien guilt (being charged with another's guilt) appears to be unfair.

52. Theories on the Nature of Sin

Theory	Source	Teaching
Dualism	Greek Philosophy and Gnosticism	Man has a spirit derived from the kingdom of light, and a body with its animal life derived from the kingdom of darkness. Sin is thus a physical evil, the defilement of the spirit by its union with a material body. Sin is to be overcome by destroying the influence of the body on the soul.
Selfishness	Strong	Sin is selfishness. It is preferring one's own ideas to God's truth. It is preferring the satisfaction of one's own will to doing God's will. It is loving oneself more than God. It may manifest itself as sensuality, unbelief, or enmity to God.
Pelagian	Pelagius	Adam's sin injured only himself. All persons are born into the world in the same state in which Adam was created. They have a knowledge of what is evil and the power to do all that God requires. Sin, therefore, consists only in the deliberate choice of evil.
Augustinian	Augustine	All persons possess an inherent, hereditary depravity, which involves both guilt and corruption. We are offensive to God's holiness because of deliberate acts of transgression and the absence of right affections. But sin is negation; it is not necessary.
Roman Catholic	Church teaching and tradition	Original sin is transmitted to all people. We are born in sin and oppressed with the corruption of our natures. This privation of righteousness allows the lower powers of man's nature to gain ascendancy over the higher, and he grows up in sin. The nature of sin is stated as the death of the soul. Sin, therefore, consists in the loss of original righteousness and the disorder of the whole of nature.
Biblical Definition	The Scriptures	The Bible uses many terms to describe the nature of sin: ignorance (Eph. 4:18), error (Mark 12:24-27), impurity, idolatry (Gal. 5:19-20), trespass (Rom. 5:15), etc. Sin's essence is placing something else in God's place. It is anything that falls short of his glory and perfection. Sin is disobedience.

53. Definition of Key Terms in Salvation

Term	Scripture	Definition
Election	Matt. 22:14; Acts 13:48; Eph. 1:4; 2 Thess. 2:13	That aspect of the eternal purpose of God whereby he certainly and eternally determines by means of unconditional and loving choice who will believe. This is not merely the intention of God to save all who may believe; rather, it determines who will believe.
Omniscience	Ps. 139:1-4; Isa.40:28; Rom. 11:33; Heb. 4:13	Relates to God's knowledge of all that is or could be. He has full knowledge of himself and all of his creation. He knows from eternity all that will occur for certain and also all that could occur.
Foreknowledge	Acts 2:23; Rom. 8:29; 11:2; Eph. 1:5	The selective knowledge of God that makes one an object of God's love; it is more than mere knowledge or cognition beforehand. The term focuses on God's motivation to act, relating to persons rather than what the persons will or will not do.
Foreordination	Eph. 1:5	God's predetermination of all things that occur in his creation, both events and a person's actions. All things that happen external to God are determined by him and are certain.
Predestination	Rom. 8:29-30	Differs from foreordination in that the former concerns the determination of all things, whereas predestination relates specifically to the determination of the elect and their conformity to the image of Christ. Predestination never occurs in the sense of one's being predestined to damnation.
Calling	*General*: Matt. 22:14; John 3:16-18 *Effectual*: John 6:44; Rom. 8: 28-30;1 Cor. 1:23-24	General: The call of the Gospel through proclamation in which all persons are invited to receive Christ. Effectual: The application of the word of the Gospel to the elect. The Holy Spirit does this work only in the elect, and this results in salvation.
Salvation	John 3:16-17; 6:37; Acts 4:12	The culmination of election: the sum total of all God's work for man in delivering him from his lost condition in sin and presenting him in glory. It is received *through* faith, but faith is *not* a *cause* or reason for which God has justified the person. The cause of God's salvation is wholly in Himself not in man (Rom. 9:12, 16).
Reprobation	Isa. 6:9-10; Rom. 9:27; 11:7	God's passive attitude in passing over some people in the bestowment of salvation. It is an expression of God's divine justice in condemning them to eternal punishment for sins.

54. Views of Salvation

Theological System	Proponents	Meaning of Salvation	Obstacle to Salvation	Means of Salvation
Liberation Theology	Gustavo Gutierrez; many Latin American Roman Catholic priests; represented through Black Theology, Feminist Theology, and Third World Theology	Deliverance from oppression	The oppression and exploitation of the powerless classes by the powerful	Politics and revolution
Existential Theology	Rudolph Bultmann Martin Heidegger	A fundamental altering of our existence, our outlook on and conduct of life. Obtaining "authentic existence" or being called by God (or the gospel) to one's true self and true destiny.	Man is imprisoned by his ego rationality and past identity-forming experiences. He is living an inauthentic existence.	Man must put to death his striving for self-gratification and security apart from God, place faith in God and be open to the future. Faith is abandoning the quest for tangible realities and transitory objects.
Secular Theology	Dietrich Bonhoeffer John A. T. Robinson Thomas J. Altizer	Salvation is moving away from religion and learning to be independent of God, coming of age, affirming oneself and getting involved in the world.	Reliance on God and religion makes man immature and lends itself to intellectual dishonesty and moral irresponsibility.	Abandoning religion and the need for God and becoming self-sufficient and fully human. This is accomplished through introspection, affirmation, and practice of scientific (e.g., antisupernatural) inquiry.
Roman Catholic Theology		Receiving grace from God through the church	Unconfessed mortal sins.	Receiving grace through participation in the sacraments of the Church.
	Second Vatican Council Karl Rahner Yves Congar Hans Küng	Receiving grace either through nature or the church. Catholics are incorporated into the Church; non-Catholic Christians are linked to the Church; non-Christians are related to the Church.		Receiving grace through either nature or the sacraments of the Church.
Evangelical Theology	Martin Luther Jonathan Edwards John Calvin	Salvation is the change of position before God, from guilty to innocent.	Sin breaks relationship with God. Man's nature is spoiled and inclines toward evil.	Being justified by faith in the finished work of Christ and receiving the Holy Spirit of God in regeneration, indwelling and sealing unto the day of redemption.

55. Salvation Terms Compared

Concept	Teaching of the Old Testament	Teaching of the New Testament
Law	God established a covenant with his people by grace. The law was simply the standard God set for those who would adhere to that covenant (Gen. 17:7).	The role of the law is not to justify, but to show us what sin is. It was a schoolmaster, to lead us to Christ (Gal. 2:16; 3:24).
Salvation	Based entirely on the work of Christ. Grace was indirectly received. Believers did not know how that grace had been effected. It was achieved by the future death of Christ. Grace was mediated by priests and sacrificial rites; it did not come about through a direct personal relationship with Christ. The Holy Spirit had not come in his fullness.	Based entirely on the work of Christ. He became a curse for us. He is the propitiation for our sins. Grace is received directly through faith, which is a gift of God. The Holy Spirit permanently indwells the believer (Rom. 3:25; Gal. 3:13; Eph. 2:8-9).
Justification	God established a covenant with his people. Although the covenant was certified by an external ritual, circumcision, that alone did not save. A circumcision of the heart was required as well (Deut. 10:16; Jer. 4:4). Nor was it the fulfillment of the law that saved; salvation came through faith. Abraham believed God, and his faith was accounted to him as righteousness (Gal. 3:6). If personal fulfillment of the law had been required, no one would have been saved.	We are justified by faith in Christ. His sacrifice satisfied God's righteous demands, and he now counts as righteous all those who trust in him (Rom. 4:5; 5:1).
Regeneration	There is no proof that O.T. saints were not regenerated. Moses identified a number of Jews who had circumcised hearts (Deut. 30:6). They were "true Jews" who were cleansed from within, having their lives altered to conform to the will of God (Rom. 2:28-29). Isaiah also described changes that resemble the New Testament depiction of the new birth (Isa. 57:15). These appear to be more than figurative.	The spiritual change wrought in a person by the Holy Spirit, by which he becomes the possessor of a new life. The change from the state of spiritual death to that of spiritual life. A change in our nature (2 Cor. 5:17; Eph. 2:1; 1 John 4:7).
Sanctification	In the Old Testament we find cases of what the New Testament terms the "fruit of the Spirit." Noah and Job were both righteous men, blameless in conduct. Special attention is given to Abraham's faith, Joseph's goodness, Moses' meekness, Solomon's wisdom, and Daniel's self-control. These believers did not have the fullness of the Holy Spirit, but enjoyed his indwelling (Ps. 51:10-12) and gifts (Exod. 36:1; Num. 11:26-30).	The work of God in developing the new life and bringing it to perfection. The separation from the sinful and setting apart for a sacred purpose. Though sanctified fully in Christ, we are gradually becoming experientially what we are positionally (Rom. 6:11; 12:1; 1 Cor. 1:2).

56. The Application of Salvation in Time

Aspect	Description	Scripture
The effectual call of God	God's special calling of the elect into fellowship with Jesus Christ	Rom. 8:30; 1 Cor. 1:9
Regeneration by the Holy Spirit	The cleansing and renewing work of the Holy Spirit imparting new life to man and enabling him to believe	John 3:5-8; 2 Cor. 5:17; Titus 3:5
Conversion through faith in Christ and repentance of sins	The unbelievers' turning away from sin and turning toward Christ	Luke 24:46-47; John 3:16; Acts 2:38
Justification by faith	The action of pronouncing sinners righteous	Rom. 3:21; 4:5; 8:33-34
Adoption as children of the heavenly Father	The transfer of the believer from alienation from God to sonship	John 1:12; Gal. 4:4-5; Eph. 1:5
Sanctification for the purpose of doing good works	The continuing work of God in the life of the believer, making him holy	Titus 2:14; Heb. 13:21; 1 Peter 5:10
Perseverance in the Word of Christ	The impossibility of the true believer's totally and finally falling away from grace, and his continuance in faith until death	John 6:39; 10:27-30; Heb. 4:14; 1 Peter 1:3-5
Glorification with Christ at his return	The complete and final redemption of the whole person conformed to the image of Christ	John 14:16-17; Rom. 8:29-30; Phil. 3:21; 1 John 1:3

57. Traditional Arguments on Election

Arminianism	

Arguments For	Arguments Against
God desires all persons to be saved and does not desire the death of the wicked (Ezek. 33:11; 1 Tim. 2:3-4; 2 Peter 3:9).	God has selected some to be saved, not all; and he has even chosen not to reveal some truths to some people (Matt. 13:10-16; John 10:24-30).
The universal character of God's commands and exhortations reveal his desire to save all people (John 3:3, 5-7; 1 Peter 1:16). Also God issues a universal invitation for all to come to Christ (Isa. 55:1; Matt. 11:28; John 9:37-39).	God's standard does not change because of man's inability to obey; a person can come to God only if God draws him (John 6:35-40, 44-47, 65).
All people are able to believe and be saved, because God has issued a universal call to salvation and because God has given all people prevenient grace to counteract sin and to render everyone able to respond to the gospel. There is no need for special grace from God for salvation.	The term "prevenient grace" is not found in the Bible. Paul expresses the fact that man is unable to turn to God and does not even seek God, but that he rejects the revelation he has been given (Rom. 1:18-32; 3:10-19).
It would be unjust of God to hold people responsible for what they are unable to do.	"Foreknowledge," as used in Scripture, is not just knowledge of future events, but is a relational term showing that God has loved and related to the elect before they came into existence and chose them to be saved because he chose to love them, regardless of their deeds (Rom. 9:26-29).
God does choose some to salvation and pass over others, because he has foreseen who will accept the offer of salvation in Christ. Foreknowledge is God's knowing beforehand who will receive salvation and is closely tied with election (Rom. 8:29; 1 Peter 1:1-2).	

57. Traditional Arguments on Election (continued)

Calvinism

Arguments For	Arguments Against
The whole human race is lost in sin, and each individual is totally corrupted in intellect, will, and emotions by sin. Man is unable to respond to God's offer of salvation because he is spiritually dead (Jer. 17:9; John 6:44; Rom. 3:1-23; 2 Cor. 4:3-4; Eph. 2:1-3).	If man is unable to respond and cannot obey God, then how can God truly offer salvation to all through the Gospel and expect obedience from man (Matt. 11:28-30; John 3:16; 6:35)?
God is sovereign in all he does, and he does all according to his good will and pleasure. He is not answerable to man, because he is the Creator and can choose whomever he wills to save (Rom. 9:20-21; Eph. 1:5; Phil. 2:13; Rev. 4:11).	God desires everyone to be saved (1 Tim. 2:3-4; 2 Peter 3:9).
God has chosen certain people for his special grace, irrespective of their physical descent, character, or good deeds. Specifically in salvation, he has chosen to save certain people through faith in Christ (John 6:37, 44, 65; 15:16; Acts 13:48; Rom. 9:6-24; Eph. 1:4-5).	God would not be fair in choosing only some to eternal life and passing over others, because this would violate man's free will to choose and because the offer of the Gospel to all would not be in good faith.
Election is an expression of God's sovereign will and is the cause of faith (Eph. 2:8-10).	God cannot demand that man believe if faith comes from him.
Election is certainly effective for the salvation of all the elect. Those whom God chooses will certainly come to faith in Christ (Rom. 8:29-30).	There is the possibility that those who have come to faith may fall from grace and lose their salvation.
Election is from all eternity and is immutable (Eph. 1:4, 9-11).	God foresaw those who would believe and elected them in eternity (Rom. 8:29).

58. Major Evangelical Views of Election

	Arminianism	Calvinism	Moderate Calvinism
Definition	The conditional choice of God by which he determined who would believe based on his foreknowledge of who *will* exercise faith. It is the *result* of man's faith.	The unconditional and loving choice of God by which he determines who *must* believe. It is the *cause* of man's faith.	The unconditional and loving choice of God by which he determines who *will* believe. It is the *cause* of man's faith.
Notable Adherents	Jacobus Arminius, John Wesley	John Calvin, Charles Spurgeon	Millard J. Erickson
Historical Roots	In the early 17th century, the Dutch pastor Arminius, while attempting to defend Beza's view, became convinced that Beza and Calvin were wrong. Wesley later went beyond Arminius by emphasizing prevenient grace.	During the Reformation, Calvin picked up on Augustine's emphasis on God's irresistible grace, man's sin nature, and predestination. Calvin was succeeded by Beza, who went a step further.	Primarily a recent interpretation.
Pros	*Emphasizes the responsibility of man to make a choice.* Also acknowledges man's depravity and helplessness without God's intervention. Most attractive aspect is its allowance for man's free will to choose. Man can resist God's grace.	*Emphasizes the holiness and sovereignty of God* and thus his right to make such decrees as election to salvation. Rightly emphasizes the total depravity of man and his inability to choose what is right unaided. The overriding doctrine is the absolute sovereignty of God, who is not dependent on the whim or will of man. Man cannot resist God's grace. This view is supported by an overwhelming amount of Scriptural evidence.	*Emphasizes the holiness and sovereignty of God while at the same time preserving the idea of man's responsibility.* God's grace is irresistible but only because God has chosen to make it so appealing to the elect that they will accept it. In other words, God enables the elect to want his grace. Thus God works his sovereign will through the will of the elect. Strikes a *balanced* position between traditional Calvinism and Arminianism.
Cons	*Deemphasizes God's sovereignty.* By putting God in a position of dependence on the decisions of a created being, this view makes it appear that God is not in control of his universe. Also, acknowledging the doctrine of total depravity required Wesley to come up with prevenient grace, which has no basis in Scripture.	*Deemphasizes man's responsibility.* Seems to eclipse man's free will and thus his responsibility for his sin. Critics charge that it is fatalistic and destroys motive for evangelism. Biggest problem: apparent logical contradiction to human freedom.	*Lacks a clear precedent* in church history. Borders on semantical dodging when it distinguishes between God's rendering something certain and something necessary (God's deciding that something will happen as opposed to deciding that it must happen).
Scriptural Evidence	Central text: No logical treatises can be found to support the Arminian position. Thus, they appeal to the universal character of God's invitation to salvation; 1 Timothy 2:3-4 is offered as evidence that God desires all people to be saved (see also Isa. 55:1; Ezek. 33:11; Acts 17:30-31; 2 Peter 3:9).	Central text: Romans 9:6-24. This demonstrates that election is based on God's just character and his sovereignty. Therefore, he will not make an unjust decision, and he is not required to explain to man why he still finds fault with those whom he did not choose.	No central text is specifically offered. Erickson bases his position on the strengths of the Calvinist position and the weakness of the Arminian and is motivated by the apparent contradiction of God's sovereignty and man's free will. He would lean to the Calvinist position in most passages.

59. Order of the Decrees

Supralapsarian (Limited Atonement)	Infralapsarian (Limited Atonement)	Amyraldian (Unlimited Atonement)	Lutheran	Wesleyan	Roman Catholic
Creation of man with a view to electing some to eternal life and damning others to eternal perdition	Permission of fall of man results in guilt, corruption, total inability.	Permission of fall of man results in corruption, guilt, moral inability.	Permission of fall of man results in guilt, corruption, total inability.	Permission of fall of man results in guilt, corruption, total inability.	Permission of fall of man results in loss of supernatural righteousness.
Permission of fall of man results in guilt, corruption, total inability	Election of some to life in Christ	Gift of Christ to render salvation possible to all	Gift of Christ to render satisfaction for sins of world	Gift of Christ to render satisfaction for sins of world	Gift of Christ to render satisfaction for all human sins
Gift of Christ to redeem the elect	Gift of Christ to redeem the elect	Election of some for gift of moral ability	Gift of means of grace to communicate saving grace	Remission of original sin to all and gift of sufficient grace to all	Institution of church, the sacraments, to apply satisfaction of Christ
Gift of the Holy Spirit to save the redeemed	Gift of the Holy Spirit to save the redeemed	Gift of the Holy Spirit to work moral ability in the elect	Predestination to life of those who do not resist the means of grace	Predestination of life of those who improve sufficient grace	Application of satisfaction of Christ through sacraments, under operation of second causes
Sanctification of all the redeemed and regenerated	Sanctification of all the redeemed and regenerated	Sanctification by the Spirit	Sanctification through the means of grace	Sanctification of all who cooperate with sufficient grace	Building up in holy life of all to whom the sacraments are communicated

Adapted from Benjamin B. Warfield, *The Plan of Salvation* (Reprint. Grand Rapids: Eerdmans, 1977), p. 31.

60. The Five Points of Calvinism and Arminianism

Category TULIP	Arminianism	Calvinism
Total Depravity	**1. Free Will or Human Ability** Although human nature was seriously affected by the fall, man has not been left in a state of total spiritual helplessness. God graciously enables every sinner to repent and believe, but he does not interfere with man's freedom. Each sinner possesses a free will, and his eternal destiny depends on how he uses it. Man's freedom consists in his ability to choose good over evil in spiritual matters; his will is not enslaved to his sinful nature. The sinner has the power either to cooperate with God's Spirit and be regenerated or to resist God's grace and perish. The lost sinner needs the Spirit's assistance, but he does not have to be regenerated by the Spirit before he can believe, for faith is man's act and precedes the new birth. Faith is the sinner's gift to God; it is man's contribution to salvation.	**1. Total Inability or Total Depravity** Because of the fall, man is unable of himself to savingly believe the Gospel. The sinner is dead, blind, and deaf to the things of God; his heart is sinful and desperately corrupt. His will is not free, it is in bondage to his evil nature, therefore he will not—indeed he cannot—choose good over evil in the spiritual realm. Consequently it takes much more than the Spirit's assistance to bring a sinner to Christ--it takes regeneration by which the Spirit makes the sinner alive and gives him a new nature but is itself a part of God's gift of salvation. Salvation is God's gift to the sinner, not the sinner's gift to God.
Uncondi-tional Election	**2. Conditional Election** God's choice of certain individuals to salvation before the foundation of the world was based on his foreseeing that they would respond to his call. He selected only those whom he knew would of themselves freely believe the Gospel. Election therefore was determined by or conditioned on what a person would do. The faith which God foresaw and upon which he based his choice was not given to the sinner by God (it was not created by the regenerating power of the Holy Spirit) but resulted from man's free will, cooperating the Spirit's working. God chose those whom he knew would, of their own free will, choose Christ. In this sense God's election is conditional.	**2. Unconditional Election** God's choice of certain individuals to salvation before the foundation of the world rested solely in his own sovereign will. His choice of particular sinners was not based on any foreseen response or obedience on their part, such as faith, repentance, etc. On the contrary, God gives faith and repentance to each individual whom he selected. These acts are the result, not the cause, of God's choice. Election therefore was not determined by or conditioned on any virtuous quality or act foreseen in man. Those whom God sovereignly elected he brings through the power of the Spirit to a willing acceptance of Christ. Thus God's choice of the sinner, not the sinner's choice of Christ, is the ultimate cause of salvation.

60. The Five Points (continued)

Category	Arminianism	Calvinism
	3. Universal Redemption, or General Atonement	**3. Particular Redemption, or Limited Atonement**
Limited Atonement	Christ's redeeming work made it possible for everyone to be saved but did not actually secure the salvation of anyone. Although Christ died for all people and for every person, only those who believe on him are saved. His death enabled God to pardon sinners on the condition that they believe, but it did not actually put away anyone's sins. Christ's redemption becomes effective only if a person chooses to accept it.	Christ's redeeming work was intended to save the elect only and actually secured salvation for them. In addition to putting away the sins of his people, Christ's redemption secured everything necessary for their salvation, including faith, which unites them to him. The gift of faith is infallibly applied by the Spirit to all for whom Christ died, therefore guaranteeing their salvation.
	4. The Holy Spirit Able to Be Effectually Resisted	**4. The Efficacious Call of the Spirit, or Irresistible Grace**
Irresistible Grace	The Spirit calls inwardly all those who are called outwardly by the Gospel invitation; he does all that he can to bring every sinner to salvation. But inasmuch as man is free, he can successfully resist the Spirit's call. The Spirit cannot regenerate the sinner until he believes; faith (which is man's contribution) precedes and makes possible the new birth. Thus man's free will limits the Spirit in the application of Christ's saving work. The Holy Spirit can draw to Christ only those who allow him to have his way with them. Until the sinner responds, the Spirit cannot give life. God's grace, therefore, is not invincible; it can be, and often is, resisted and thwarted by men.	In addition to the outward general call to salvation, which is made to everyone who hears the Gospel, the Holy Spirit extends to the elect a special inward call that inevitably brings them to salvation. The external call (which is made to all without distinction) can be, and often is, rejected; whereas the internal call (which is made only to the elect) cannot be rejected; it always results in conversion. By means of this special call the Spirit irresistibly draws sinners to Christ. He is not limited in His work of applying salvation to man's will, nor is he dependent on man's cooperation for success. The Spirit graciously causes the elect sinner to cooperate, to believe, to repent, to come freely and willingly to Christ. God's grace, therefore, is invincible; it never fails to result in the salvation of those to whom it is extended.
	5. Falling From Grace	**5. Perseverance of the Saints**
Perseverance of the Saints	Those who believe and are truly saved can lose their salvation by failing to keep up their faith. Not all Arminians agree on this point; some hold that believers are eternally secure in Christ—that once a sinner is regenerated, he can never be lost.	All who are chosen by God, redeemed by Christ, and given faith by the Spirit are eternally saved. They are kept in faith by the power of Almighty God and thus persevere to the end.
	Rejected by the Synod of Dort This was the system of thought contained in the "Remonstrance" (though the "five points" were not originally arranged in this order). It was submitted by the Arminians to the Church of Holland in 1610 for adoption but was rejected by the Synod of Dort in 1619 on the ground that it was unscriptural.	**Reaffirmed by the Synod of Dort** This system of theology was reaffirmed by the Synod of Dort in 1619 as the doctrine of salvation contained in the Holy Scriptures. The system was at that time formulated into "five points" (in answer to the five points submitted by the Arminians) and has ever since been known as "the five points of Calvinism."

61. Different Views on the Means of Grace

Reformed	Arminian	Lutheran	Roman Catholic
Saving Faith by Efficacious Grace	Saving Faith by Common Grace	Baptism and the Eucharist	Baptism, the Eucharist and Other Sacraments
faith without means		faith through faith	means without faith
			(*ex opere operato*) operation by physical contact

62. General Versus Effectual Calling

	General Calling	Effectual Calling
Definition	It involves the presentation of the Gospel in which the individual is offered the promise of salvation in Christ and invited to accept Christ by faith in order to receive the forgiveness of sins and eternal life.	It involves the general calling of God in the Gospel made effective in an individual as he or she believes the Gospel and accepts Christ as Savior and Lord.
Agent	Issued by the Father to all who hear the Gospel; mediated especially through believers empowered by the Holy Spirit of God as they communicate the Gospel as revealed in the Word of God.	It is issued by the Father and made effective by the work of the Holy Spirit as he illuminates and enables the individual to understand and respond positively to the Gospel of the Lord Jesus as contained in the Word of God.
Subjects & Examples	It is for all people but heard only by those who hear the Gospel "Many are called but few are chosen" (Matt. 22:14).	It is given only to all of the elect. Saul - Acts 9:1-19; Lydia - Acts 16:14; Romans 8:30
Purpose	It reveals the great love of God to sinners in general. It reveals God's holiness and righteousness.	Because of mans's total depravity, it is absolutely necessary in order to bring the elect to faith and conversion.
Results	It does not necessarily result in salvation. It can be rejected, resulting in the sinner's condemnation.	Since it is effectual and irrevocable, it necessarily results in salvation. It is impossible to reject.
Timing	It is prior to conversion and may or may not lead to it.	It is logically prior to conversion and necessarily leads to it.

63. The Seven Roman Catholic Sacraments

Sacrament	Procedure	Significance	Vatican II Emphasis
Baptism	Priest performs the rite on infants.	Produces rebirth, "infant Christian." Necessary for salvation. Frees one from original sin and guilt. Unites one to Christ and the church.	Baptism to receive greater emphasis. Convert to receive instruction beforehand. Illustrates commitment to Christ. Emphasizes unity of all members in Christ.
Confirmation	Bishop lays hands on person whereby the person confirmed receives the Holy Spirit.	Necessary sequence after baptism. With baptism, part of the "sacrament of initiation." Person receives the Holy Spirit, bringing one to maturity and dedication.	Endeavor to unite baptism and confirmation as one act of initiation. Separating the two sacraments suggests there are degrees of membership in the church.
Eucharist	Priest celebrates the Mass. Upon his pronouncing, "This is my body," the bread and wine become the body and blood of Christ.	The Mass is ongoing sacrifice of Christ. Same as Calvary, except the Mass is not bloody. In the Mass, Christ offers atonement for sin. Participant receives forgiveness from venial sins. Eating the bread is eating Christ.	Frequent participation encouraged to increase "union with Christ." Ceremony now involves lay people. Shorter, simpler ceremony; more use of Scripture.
Confession (Penance)	Three steps: 1. Sorrow for sin 2. Oral confession to priest 3. Absolution of sins by priest	Having confessed all known sins to priest and stated intention not to sin in the future, adherent receives absolution from sins by priest.	New view of sin: distorted personal relationship and motives. Allows for general confession and absolution. General confession performed in service of singing, Scripture, prayer, sermon, self-examination, confession, absolution.
Holy Orders	Ordination to office: bishop, priest, deacon. As successor to the apostles, bishop ordains priest.	Confers on recipient the priestly power to mediate grace through sacraments such as offering the body and blood of Christ to remit sins. Priest mediates between God and men as Christ mediated between God and men.	Greater involvement of lay people in ministry. Laypeople to develop and use gifts in church. Reduced distinction between priest and people. Priest considered "brother among brothers."
Marriage	Vows are exchanged in presence of a priest.	Sign of union of Christ and church. Indissoluble because marriage of Christ and the church is indissoluble.	Marriage is not only for procreation. Greater emphasis on love in marriage. Mass permitted at weddings with baptized non-Catholics.
Anointing the sick	Bishop consecrates oil. Person near death anointed by priest.	Removes infirmity and obstacles left by sin, which prevent the soul from entering glory. Prepares people for death by strengthening grace in the soul.	Broadened usage: changed from "extreme unction" to "anointing the sick." Used to strengthen/heal body and soul. Sick person shares in readings, prayers.

64. Views of the Atonement

	Ransom to Satan Theory	Recapitulation Theory	Dramatic Theory	Mystical Theory	Example Theory
Definition	Christ's death was a ransom paid to Satan to purchase captive man from Satan's claims.	Christ in his life recapitulated all the stages of human life, in so doing reversed the course initiated by Adam.	Christ is Victor in a divine conflict of good and evil and wins man's release from bondage.	Christ took on a human, sinful nature but through the power of the Holy Spirit triumphed over it. A knowledge of this will mystically influence man.	Christ's death provided an example of faith and obedience to inspire man to be obedient.
Proponents	Origen	Irenaeus	Aulen	Schleiermacher	Pelagius, Socinus, Abelard
Scriptural Support	Matthew 20:28; Mark 10:45; I Corinthians 6:20	Romans 5:15-21; Hebrews 2:10	Matthew 20:28; Mark 10:45; I Corinthians 15:51-57	Hebrews 2:10, 14-18; 4:14-16	I Peter 2:21; I John 2: 6
Object	Satan	Satan	Satan	Man	Man
Man's Spiritual Condition	Bondage to Satan	Bondage to Satan	Bondage to Satan	Lack of God-consciousness	Spiritually alive (Pelagian)
Meaning of Christ's Death	God's victory over Satan	Christ's recapitulation of all of the stages of human life	God's victory over Satan	Christ's triumph over his own sinful nature	An example of true faith and obedience
Value to Man	Freedom from enslavement to Satan	Reversing the course of mankind from disobedience to obedience	God's reconciliation of the world out of its bondage to evil	A mystical subconscious influence	Inspiration to a faithful and obedient life

64. Views of the Atonement (continued)

	Moral Influence Theory	Commercial Theory	Governmental Theory	Penal Substitution Theory
Definition	Christ's death demonstrated God's love, which causes man's heart to soften and repent.	Christ's death brought infinite honor to God. So God gave Christ a reward which he did not need, and Christ passed it on to man.	Christ's death demonstrates God's high regard for his law. It shows God's attitude toward sin. Through Christ's death God has a rationale to forgive the sins of those who repent and accept Christ's substitutionary death.	Christ's death was a vicarious (substitutionary) sacrifice that satisfied the demands of God's justice upon sin, paying the penalty of man's sin, bringing forgiveness, imputing righteousness, and reconciling man to God.
Proponents	Abelard, Bushnell, Rashdall	Anselm	Grotius	Calvin
Scriptural Support	Romans 5:8; 2 Corinthians 5:17-19; Philippians 2:5-11; Colossians 3:24	John 10:18	Psalm 2, 5; Isaiah 42:21	John 11:50-52; Romans 5:8-9; Titus 2:14; I Peter 3:18,
Object	Man	God/Man	God/Man	God
Man's Spiritual Condition	Man is sick and needs help.	Man is dishonoring to God.	Man is a violator of God's moral law.	Man is totally depraved.
Meaning of Christ's Death	Demonstrated God's love toward man.	Brought infinite honor to God.	A substitute for the penalty of sin and showed God's attitude toward sin.	Christ bore the penalty of sin instead of man.
Value to Man	Man is moved to accept God's forgiveness by seeing God's love for man.	This honor, not needed by Christ, is applied to sinners for salvation.	Makes legal God's desire to forgive those who accept Christ as their substitute.	Through his repentance, man can accept Christ's substitution as payment for sin.

65. The Extent of the Atonement

Unlimited Atonement

Statement of View	The death of Christ was sufficient for all people, but efficient for a limited number.

Support	Objections
Numerous verses seem to indicate that the death of Christ was for the whole of mankind. The major two verses are 1 Timothy 4:10 and 1 John 2:2. These state that Christ is the propitiation and the Savior of the world. Other verses are Isaiah 53:6; John 1:29; I Timothy 2:6; Titus 2:11; Hebrews 2:9.	The words "all" and "whole" do not always refer to the totality of its contents. An example is the taxing of the whole world by Caesar; this did not include the Japanese. The whole world in these verses means people of every geographical area.
The universal proclamation of the Gospel is based on the unlimited atonement of Christ. In order for the Gospel to be sincerely offered to all mankind, Christ had to have died for all mankind (Matt. 24:14; 28:19; Acts 1:8; 17:30).	The proclamation of the Gospel is based on the finished work of Christ. The elect are throughout the world, and they need to hear the Gospel in order to be saved. The taking of the Gospel is a matter of obedience, not unlimited atonement.
The love of God is toward the whole world and whoever believes is saved. Therefore, the extent of Christ's death is to all people.	The love of God is toward a special group, as seen in his love of Israel (Amos 3:2). His love is toward the elect of every geographical area of the world. Those that believe are those God has given to the Son (John 6:37-40).
The work of Christ is sufficient to secure the salvation of the elect but is secured by means of faith (Rom. 10:17).	If the death of Christ was all-sufficient, faith becomes unnecessary and meaningless.
The natural benefits of the world are also enjoyed by the nonelect. These benefits include sunshine, rain, good health, etc.	The natural benefits are a result of God's common grace. These things are given from God because of his character. He can be kind to whom he wishes.

Limited Definite Atonement

Statement of View	Christ's coming was not to provide salvation for all mankind, but to render certain the salvation of the elect.

Support	Objections
Those who advocate a limited atonement say that God provided salvation only for his people (Matt. 1:21), his sheep (John 10:15, 26), his friends (John 15:13), the church (Acts 20:28), and the bride (Eph. 5:25).	The atonement will not save all men, but is available for all. These verses refer to those whom God chose. It is these that have made the atonement efficient.
Those for whom Christ died are those whom the Father gave to him (John 6:37-40). Christ did not die for those whom the Father did not give him. Therefore, it was for a certain number that he died.	These verses do not mention a limited atonement. That only a certain number are chosen is evident because not all will be saved.
Christ died for the elect in every area of the world. This is what the Scripture means when it says that Christ died for the whole world (1 Tim. 4:10; 1 John 2:2).	That the death of Christ was for all mankind makes more sense than that he died for people of every geographical area.
What connection does the death of Christ have with the nonelect? If he died for all, why are some people not saved?	The death of Christ makes potential the salvation of all, but it will be actual only to a certain number. This is the only connection; those who reject this must bear the consequences.
The intercessory work of Christ was for his own. Since he prayed only for a certain group, he intended to provide salvation for a limited number.	Only a certain number will actually be saved. Christ knew who these would be and these are the people he prayed for.
The work of Christ is said to be for specific groups: Paul, Israel, the church. This shows that his work is not unlimited in scope.	His salvation is made actual to certain groups, but he died for all. The groups who realize salvation are only a subset of those for whom he died.

66. The Penal Substitution Theory of the Atonement

	Necessity	Substitution	Propitiation	Imputation
Explained	God cannot merely overlook man's sin, nor can he just forgive man without requiring that payment be made or punishment be given for sin. In this sense, the atonement is necessary for man to be made right with his Creator.	The normal meaning of the word is to be taken in this context. It simply means that the atonement is a sacrifice offered in place of the sinner. Thus the sacrifice bears the sinner's guilt.	To regain favor or appease God. To satisfy his demands, and thereby divert his anger. Man's sin does not just make God sad, it makes him angry. His anger, or wrath, can be satisfied only by the execution of his justice. His judicial system cannot be short-circuited.	While substitution and propitiation have to do with negative aspects of the atonement (what God has taken away from us), imputation has to do with the positive aspect of the atonement (what God has given to us). God has taken away the guilt of believers, but he has also imputed to them the righteousness of Christ.
Scripture Reference	Hebrews 9:22	John 1:29; 2 Corinthians 5:21; Galatians 3:13	Leviticus 4:35; Romans 3:25-26; 5:9	Romans 6:3-4
Objection	Why does God not simply forgive us as an act of good will instead of requiring a payment?	Is it not improper and unjust to penalize an innocent party?	Doesn't the appeasement of the Father by the Son reveal conflict within the Godhead?	Is it not improper and unfair to reward a guilty party?
Response to Objection	Even if God could overlook sin against himself as an act of good will, he is still bound by his nature to preserve justice in the universe. To ignore sin would destroy the meaningfulness of the concept of justice. Also, humans may simply forgive other humans as an act of good will because we are imperfect and in desperate need of forgiveness ourselves. But God is perfect and does not need forgiveness. Consequently, the parallel between man's and God's forgiveness breaks down.	The answer to this question is yes unless the innocent party receives the penalty voluntarily and the judge is inseparable from the innocent party. Jesus meets both of these requirements. He gave his life willingly (John 10:17-18) and he was inseparable from the Father. Thus in effect, the Judge punished himself.	The answer to this question may be put in the form of another question: Can a person be angry and loving at the same time? Any parent knows that the answer is yes. The Father was angry over the world's sin, but he loved the world so much that he sent his Son to atone for the sin of man. Thus the Father did not change from an angry God to a loving God when Christ died on the cross. God's love was there all the time and was in fact the motivation for the atonement. His holiness demanded a payment for sin. His love provided the payment.	This question is the other side of the objection to substitution. It doesn't seem fair that an innocent party is punished and likewise, it doesn't seem fair that a guilty party is rewarded. Yet that is what happens in the atonement. But the reason that God sees this transaction as absolutely just is that when we put our faith in him, we become united with Christ. In a sense, we become married, inseparable, so that it is not a transfer of righteousness as much as holding it in common. It is shared.
Implications About God's Character	Emphasis on God's sovereignty and position of official administrator of the judicial system of the universe.	Emphasis on God's love for his creation. He defines love by his nature. Real love always demands personal sacrifice.	Emphasis on God's absolute holiness and justifiable anger over sin. He deserves respect and absolute obedience and vents his wrath on ungodliness.	Emphasis on God's desire for intimate fellowship with his creation. Because of the atonement we are heirs of the Father and joint-heirs with Son.

67. Results of the Death of Christ

The Avoidance of Divine Judgments

God views sin as judged in the death of his Son. The believer is sheltered under the redeeming blood of Christ (Rom. 2:4-5; 4:17; 9:22; 1 Peter 3:20; 2 Peter 3:9, 15).

Took Away Sins Covered by Sacrifice Before the Cross

Sins committed between the time of Adam and Christ's death on the cross were covered by sacrifice. In Christ they were taken away (Acts 17:30; Rom. 3:25; Heb. 9:15; 10:2-26).

National Salvation of Israel

The future Israel of faith will have its sins removed (Rom. 9-11, esp. 11:25-29).

Millennial and Eternal Blessings Upon the Gentiles

Millennial earthly blessings, which are assured to Israel, will be shared by the Gentiles (Matt. 25:31-46; Acts 15:17; Rev. 21:24).

The Spoiling of Principalities and Powers

Christ gained direct legal victory at the cross over Satan and his hosts (John 12:31, 16:11; Eph. 1:21; Col. 2:14-15).

The Ground of Peace

The cross brought peace between God and man (Rom. 5:1; Eph. 2:13-14a; Col. 1:20), between Jew and Gentile (Eph. 2:14-18; Col. 3:11), and universal peace (1 Cor. 15:27-28; Eph. 2:14-15; Col. 1:20).

The Purification of Things in Heaven

Heavenly "things" were purified on the ground of Christ's blood (Heb. 9:23-24).

Substitution for Sinners

Jesus took *our* place; he bore the penalty for *our* sins (Luke 22:19-20; John 3:36; 6:51; 15:13; Eph. 1:3; Heb. 2:9; 1 Peter 3:18; 1 John 5:11-12).

The Fulfillment of the Law

Jesus' imputed righteousness becomes the believer's righteousness before God as perfect fulfillment of the law (Acts 15:10; Rom 1:16-17; 3:21-22, 31; 4:5, 11, 13-16, 23-24; 5:19;10:4; 2 Cor. 5:21; Gal. 3:8; 4:19-31; 5:1).

Redemption From Sin

God himself paid the ransom of human sin through the death of his Son (Acts 20:28; Rom. 3:23-24).

Reconciliation of Man to God

God's attitude toward the world has changed completely (Rom. 5:10-11; 2 Cor. 5:18-20; Eph. 2:16; Col. 1:20-22).

Propitiation Toward God

God's righteousness and law have been vindicated (satisfied) (Rom. 3:25; Heb. 4:16; 1 John 2:2; 4:10).

Judgment of the Sin Nature

The sin nature was judged at the cross and is now able to be controlled by the Spirit in the believer's life. The believer positionally shares with Christ his crucifixion, death, burial, and resurrection.

Forgiveness and Cleansing

The believer in Jesus has forgiveness and cleansing in both justification and sanctification through Christ's blood and continuing advocacy in heaven (1 John 1:1-2:2).

68. Varieties of Universalism

Universal Reconciliation (cf. some Barthians)	Maintains that Christ's death accomplished its purpose of reconciling all mankind to God. Whatever separation exists between man and the benefits of God's grace is subjective in nature, existing only in man's mind. Reconciliation is an accomplished fact.
Universal Pardon (cf. C. H. Dodd)	Maintains that God, being loving, will not hold unswervingly to the conditions he has laid down. Though threatening eternal punishment he will in the end relent and forgive everyone. God will treat all persons as if they had believed.
Universal Restoration (cf. Origen)	At some point in the future all things will be restored to their original and intended state. Full salvation may be preceded by cycles of reincarnation or by some purgatorial period at the beginning of the life hereafter.
The Doctrine of a Second Chance	The work of Christ is sufficient to secure the salvation of the elect, but salvation is effectually secured by the means of faith (Rom. 10:10-13). All people, even those who have heard and rejected, will be confronted with the claims of Christ in the life to come. Everyone given such an opportunity will of course accept it.
Universal Temporal Blessings	The natural benefits of the world are also enjoyed by everyone. These benefits include sunshine, rain, good health, etc., and are a result of God's common grace. These things are given from God because of his character.

Arguments For	Arguments Against
It is ridiculous to think that a living, all-powerful, and sovereign God could create a system whereby a portion of mankind (the epitome of his creation) would be condemned to everlasting punishment.	God will not do anything that contradicts any of his attributes. Hence in order to harmonize his perfect love and perfect justice, he devised the biblically explained system of redemption. We must accept the biblical record, not our own finite reasoning.
To condemn the unsaved to everlasting punishment as a result of their relatively short life span on earth is unjust.	God is the final standard of justice, not man.
If an all-powerful and sovereign God desires all people to be saved (1 Tim. 2: 3-4; 2 Peter 3:9), then surely all are saved.	Although God desires salvation for all mankind, a person must respond to God's offer of salvation and many do not (John 5:40).
Christ's death has acquitted all mankind of their condemnation before God, just as Adam brought the entire human race into sin (Rom. 5:18; I Cor. 15:22).	The context of both verses clearly shows that the benefits of Christ's death are for those in Christ, just as the penalties of Adam's sin are for those in Adam.

68. Varieties of Universalism (continued)

Arguments For	Arguments Against
The theme of the New Testament is that of God's sovereign love. If his love is sovereign, it must be completely victorious. To say that God's love is not adequate to secure the salvation of all mankind in the end presumes a finite God.	Agreed, God has infinite love, but he also has justice and holiness. He has already devised a plan consistent with all his infinite attributes. It is up to man to accept God's plan, instead of devising his own plan and calling God unjust if he does not accept it.
Christ paid the penalty of sin on behalf of all mankind (Heb. 2:9), and legally, if such an adequate substitution is made and accepted, it is unjust for the creditor to the require the original payment also.	The substitutionary death of Christ was sufficient for the salvation of all (2 Cor. 5:19); however, each person must believe in order for it to be effectual on his behalf (v. 20).
God's all-encompassing attribute is love. His judgment is only a temporary measure to reform unrepentant persons, and hence is itself motivated by love. Ultimately all people will be reformed, whether in this life or the after-life, and hence ultimately all will be saved.	Scripture never refers to the abode of unbelievers after death as a place for reformation. It is always referred to as a place of destruction and punishment ((Matt. 25:46; Luke 16:19-31). The only reference to any encounter of Christ with unbelievers after their death is in 1 Peter 3:19, and this passage is at most applicable only to the unbelievers of Noah's day.
Ultimately all mankind will believe, whether in this life or the hereafter (Phil. 2:10-11; 1 Peter 3:19, 20).	Christ's death made all people saveable (2 Cor. 5:19), But man must believe in order to be saved (v. 20).
Many will not believe in this life, but the after-life offers a second chance.	The constant scriptural references to "saving faith" clearly indicate that some will not believe (John 1:11-12; 3:18: 20:31).
	The words of Jesus indicate clearly that some go to eternal life and others to eternal punishment. Further, in Matthew 25:46, the word for eternal is *aionos*, meaning "relating to the final order of things which shall not pass away."
Warnings of "lostness" are merely hypothetical and constitute one of the ways in which God secures the universal salvation of all mankind.	Other New Testament Scriptures point to the destruction of the nonelect (Rom. 9:22; 2 Thess. 1:9; Rev. 21:8).
	Christ and the apostles were constantly warning people of God's wrath and judgment on sin and urgently calling them to repentance. Hence, if universalism is true, Christ and the apostles were either ignorant or grossly deceptive.

69. Views of Sanctification

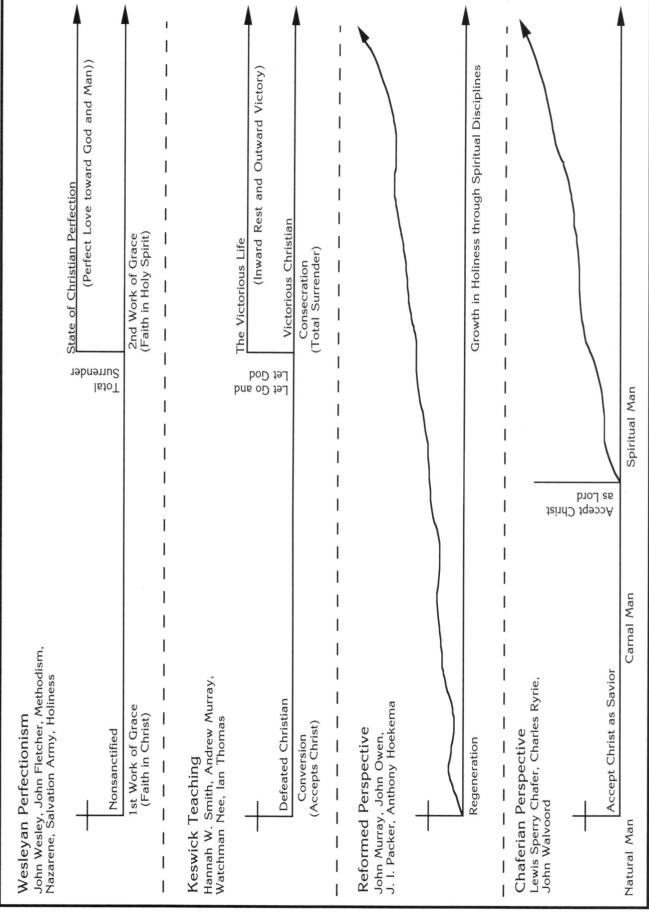

Wesleyan Perfectionism
John Wesley, John Fletcher, Methodism, Nazarene, Salvation Army, Holiness

Natural Man | Nonsanctified | 1st Work of Grace (Faith in Christ) | Total Surrender | 2nd Work of Grace (Faith in Holy Spirit) | State of Christian Perfection (Perfect Love toward God and Man)

Keswick Teaching
Hannah W. Smith, Andrew Murray, Watchman Nee, Ian Thomas

Defeated Christian | Conversion (Accepts Christ) | Let Go and Let God | Consecration (Total Surrender) | Victorious Christian | The Victorious Life (Inward Rest and Outward Victory)

Reformed Perspective
John Murray, John Owen, J. I. Packer, Anthony Hoekema

Regeneration | Growth in Holiness through Spiritual Disciplines

Chaferian Perspective
Lewis Sperry Chafer, Charles Ryrie, John Walvoord

Natural Man | Carnal Man | Accept Christ as Savior | Accept Christ as Lord | Spiritual Man

Randy Gleason. Adapted and used by permission.

70. Five Views of Sanctification

	Beginning Point	God's Work	Man's Responsibility	Effects of Sanctification	Extent of Sanctification
Wesleyan	Sanctification begins at conversion (new birth), when a person responds to God's prevenient grace for salvation (19, 25).*	Sanctification is a work of God's grace. The Holy Spirit works to regenerate the believer's heart from one of rebellion to one of wholehearted love. After salvation (man's response to God's prevenient grace), God gives man sanctifying grace to enable him to avoid willful sin (25).	Man is obliged to follow God's will (27). He must be holy (1 Peter 1:15-16) and put on the "new self" (Eph. 4:22, 24). One can lose his salvation by continued disobedience to God. The Christian must "fulfill the law on the basis of faith" (27).	Sanctification produces love in action (27). Man is freed from the power of the law (27). The Holy Spirit communicates God's nature to believers and imparts a life of love to them; giving them a new heart, causing them to love instead of disobeying (28).	The Christian should reach a point where he does not willfully sin against God (Matt. 5:48; 6:13; John 3:8) (15). Here the struggle between good and evil ceases (17). This is a state of "entire sanctification" (17-19). Only at Christ's second coming will the believer be perfected in terms of unknown shortcomings.
Reformed	Sanctification begins at conversion through saving faith (61-62).	God renews us in his likeness by conforming us to Christ (Rom. 8:29). It is a continual process, whereby the Holy Spirit works in us (2 Cor. 3:18).	Man should follow Christ's example (67). He should serve the members of Christ's body (John 13:14-15). He should also put on the mind of Christ (Phil. 2:5-11). Man must cooperate with God's work in him, expressing gratitude for salvation (85).	The Christian no longer has his old self, which was crucified (Rom. 6:6). Through sanctification, the Christian is a genuinely new, though not a totally new person (74). Sanctification continues throughout life whereby the person is renewed. For instance, the person is able to resist sin (82). Also, God conforms the believer to his image (Rom. 8:29).	By sanctification, the believer becomes more Christlike. However, perfection is not attained in this life (84). The believer must continue to fight sin as long as he lives (Gal. 5:16-17).
Pentecostal	Holiness Pentecostals believe that a second work of the Holy Spirit sanctifies a believer in a crisis experience whereby original sin is removed entirely (108-9, 134). Other Pentecostals (e.g., Assemblies of God) claim that believers who have already received new life by the Spirit (salvation) later receive an empowering baptism of the Holy Spirit that begins a life of spiritual growth in them (193). This latter work by the Spirit is continual, and not a single crisis experience (109-10).	God produces a baptism in the Spirit (the initial work of sanctification) to produce growth (118). The blood of Christ also purifies us from sin continuously (1 John 1:7) (117). The Word of God also produces sanctification in the believer (120).	Man must cooperate with the Holy Spirit, presenting himself to God (Rom. 12:1-2) (120). We should constantly obey God (126). This involves putting to death sinful things that belong to our earthly nature (1 Thess. 4:3-4) (117).	Sanctification is both positional and progressive (113-14). Sanctification is instantaneous in that it immediately sets the believer apart from sin unto God (Col. 2:11-12)(115-16). Sanctification is also progressive, whereby God keeps on cleansing us from sin (1 John 1:7) (117).	The goal of sanctification is "entire sanctification," whereby the believer attains the "wholehearted desire and determination to do the will of God" (124). The believer is still tempted and still retains his old nature throughout earthly life (124).

*Numbers in parentheses indicate the page numbers in Melvin E. Dieter et. al., *Five Views on Sanctification* (Grand Rapids: Zondervan, 1987). Used by permission.

70. Five Views of Sanctification (continued)

	Beginning Point	God's Work	Man's Responsibility	Effects of Sanctification	Extent of Sanctification
Keswick	Sanctification begins upon belief (at salvation).	God (Father, Son, and Holy Spirit) comes to live with the individual believer, and renews him after the likeness of God (174).	Man should live in the Spirit to receive all of the fullness of God (Eph. 3:19). The essential focus of the Christian's life should be to have a close relationship with God (166).	The "normal" Christian (being sanctified) should have sustained victory over known sin (153). The old nature is not eradicated but is counteracted by the work of the Holy Spirit in the believer (157). Sanctification is both positional (forgiveness, justification, regeneration [new life received]), and experiential (our call to holiness, 2 Cor. 7:1). Man is still influenced by sin but not necessarily under its control (174). Man has a new potential–the ability to choose right and to do it consistently (178).	The believer will not attain to perfection in this life but should experience consistent success in overcoming sin (155). A Christian's life should be controlled by the Holy Spirit (155). Total sanctification does not occur until Christ's second coming (1 John 3:2) (160).
Augustinian-Dispensational	Sanctification begins at the time of conversion (saving faith) (205).	At regeneration (at the time of salvation), God prepares the individual for experiential sanctification (209). The baptism of the Holy Spirit places the believer in the body of Christ, enabling the believer to have fellowship, receive spiritual power, bear fruit, etc. (213). The Spirit indwells all believers and also fills those who yield to him willingly (218). Because of the Spirit's indwelling, the Christian can grow in sanctification.	Man is responsible to walk by the Spirit (continually depending on the Spirit's power) (220). Using God's power, Christians should avoid sin, which grieves the indwelling Spirit (219). We must be willing to follow God's will and direction for our lives (219). Believers today are to reflect the holiness of God as an example of God's grace (226).	The Christian has two natures: the flesh and the spirit, which are opposed to each other (Rom. 7) (203). The two natures in man are parallel to the two natures-of Christ (human and divine) (203-4). The believer receives a "new self," which is a new life springing from his new nature (Col. 3:9-10) (208).	Christians will not receive ultimate perfection until they are in heaven (Eph. 5:25-27; 1 John 3:2).

71. The Church's Foundation

View One	View Two	View Three
"The Rock" = Peter	"The Rock" = Christ	"The Rock" = the confession of Peter
Held by Tertullian, Cyprian, Vatican 1 & 11	Held by Augustine, Calvin, Zwingli	Held by Chrysostom, Zahn
Arguments for:	**Arguments for:**	**Arguments for:**
Christ was speaking to Peter when he spoke of the rock.	Passages such as 1 Corinthians 3:11; 1 Peter 2:4-8	Christ was pleased with Peter's confession (Matt. 16:16-18).
Petros (Peter) means a small rock.	*Petra* is used metaphorically of Christ in the New Testament.	Peter's confession is that on which the preaching office was established.
According to Roman Catholicism, Peter was the first pope.	Christ makes a distinction between *petros* and *petra*.	
Arguments against:	**Arguments against:**	**Arguments against:**
A distinction is made between *petros* (a small rock) and *petra* (a big rock).	Christ may not have spoken these exact words, since he spoke Aramaic.	Peter denied Christ's impending death (Matt. 16:22-23).
Peter calls Christ the foundation (1 Peter 1:4-8).	Christ never claims to be the rock.	The office of preaching was established long before Peter's confession.
Peter never claimed to be the pope.		
1 Corinthians 3:11 makes it impossible for Peter to be the foundation of the church.		

72. A Dispensational Comparison of Israel and the Church

		Israel	Church
SIMILARITIES		—NEITHER REPRESENTS THE TOTALITY OF GOD'S PROGRAM. — BOTH SHARE IN THE LARGER KINGDOM PROGRAM OF GOD. —BOTH ARE DESIGNED TO GLORIFY GOD, THOUGH IN DIFFERENT WAYS. —THERE IS A CONTINUITY BETWEEN THE TWO ENTITIES.	
D I S T I N C T I O N S	**Relation**	Relationship based on physical birth	Relationship based on spiritual birth
	Headship	Abraham	Christ
	Nationality	One nation	From all nations
	Divine Interaction	National and individual	Individual salvation but relationship in the body of Christ.
	Dispensations	From Abraham on	Restricted to this age only
	Governing Principle	Embodied in the Mosaic covenant (in the future, the new covenant)	A grace system that includes law

73. Local Church Contrasted with the Universal Church

Visible	Invisible
Membership: saved and lost	Membership: saved only
Only currently living people	Both dead and living in Christ
Many local churches	Only one universal church
Differing denominations	No single denomination
Part of the body of Christ	The entire body of Christ
Differing types of government	Christ the only head
Ministering the ordinances (or sacraments)	Ordinances fulfilled (e.g., 1 Cor. 11:23-26; Rev. 19:9)

74. Analogies of Christ and the Church

Christ	Church	Reference	Terminology
Head	Body	Colossians 1:18a	"And he is the head of the body, the church."
Cornerstone	Temple	Ephesians 2:20-21	". . . Christ Jesus himself as the chief cornerstone."
Beloved	Virgin	2 Corinthians 11:2	"I promised you to one husband, to Christ, so that I might present you as a pure virgin to him."
Bridegroom	Bride	Revelation 21:9	"'Come, I will show you the bride, the wife of the Lamb.'"
Ruler (implied)	City	Revelation 21:9-10	"He . . . showed me the Holy City, Jerusalem, coming down out of heaven from God."
Owner	People	Titus 2:14	". . . to purify for himself a people that are his very own."
Shepherd	Flock	1 Peter 5:2-4	"Be shepherds of God's flock . . . . And when the Chief Shepherd appears, you will receive the crown. . . ."
Firstborn	Household	Ephesians 2:19 Colossians 1:18b	". . . members of God's household." "He is the beginning and the firstborn."
Creator	New Man	Ephesians 2:15	"His purpose was to create in himself one new man out of the two."
Founder (implied)	Chosen People	1 Peter 2:9	"You are a chosen people . . . a holy nation, a people belonging to God."
High Priest	Royal Priesthood	Hebrews 4:14 1 Peter 2:9	"We have a great high priest . . . Jesus the Son of God." ". . . a royal priesthood. . . ."
Heir	Inheritance	Ephesians 1:18	". . . his glorious inheritance in the saints."

75. The Offices of Elder and Deacon—Qualifications and Duties

Qualifications

Elders

Qualification	Reference
Self-controlled	1 Timothy 3:2; Titus 1:8
Hospitable	1 Timothy 3:2; Titus 1:8
Able to teach	1 Timothy 3:2; 5:17; Titus 1:9
Not violent but gentle	1 Timothy 3:3; Titus 1:7
Not a lover of money	1 Timothy 3:3
Not quarrelsome	1 Timothy 3:3
Not a recent convert	1 Timothy 3:6
Having a good reputation with outsiders	1 Timothy 3:7
Not overbearing	Titus 1:7
Not quick-tempered	Titus 1:7
Loving what is good	Titus 1:8
Upright and holy	Titus 1:8
Disciplined	Titus 1:8

Deacons and Elders

Qualification	Reference
Above reproach (blameless)	1 Timothy 3:2, 9; Titus 1:6
Having one wife	1 Timothy 3:2,12; Titus 1:6
Temperate	1 Timothy 3:2, 8; Titus 1:7
Respectable	1 Timothy 3:2, 8
Not given to drunkenness	1 Timothy 3:3, 8; Titus 1:7
Able to manage his family well	1 Timothy 3:4, 12; Titus 1:6
Having obedient children	1 Timothy 3:4-5,12; Titus 1:6
Not a pursuer of dishonest gain	1 Timothy 3:8; Titus 1:7

Deacons

Qualification	Reference
Holding firmly to the deep truths	1 Timothy 3:9; Titus 1:9
Sincere	1 Timothy 3:8
Tested	1 Timothy 3:10

Duties

Elders

Duty	Reference
Administrative—to rule the church	1 Timothy 5:17; Titus 1:7
Pastoral—to shepherd the church	1 Peter 5:2; Jude 12
Educational—to teach the church	Ephesians 4:12-13; 1 Timothy 3:2
Officiative—to lead in the functions of the church	James 5:14
Representative—to represent the church	Acts 20:17; 1 Timothy 5:17

Deacons

Duty	Reference
To help the poor	Acts 6:1-6
To relieve the elders	Acts 6:1-4

76. Functional Qualifications of Elders and Deacons

Relation to God

Holding firmly to scriptural truths
1 Timothy 3;9; Titus 1;9

Upright and holy
Titus 1:8

Able to teach
1 Timothy 3:2; 5:17; Titus 1:9

Above reproach
1 Timothy 3:2, 9; Titus 1:6

Not a new convert
1 Timothy 3:6

Loving what is good
Titus 1:8

Tested
1 Timothy 3:10

Relation to Others

Sincere
1 Timothy 3:8

Respectable
1 Timothy 3:2, 8

Hospitable
1 Timothy 3:2; Titus 1:8

Not quarrelsome
1 Timothy 3:3

Not violent but gentle
1 Timothy 3:3; Titus 1:7

Good reputation with outsiders
1 Timothy 3:7

Not overbearing
Titus 1:7

Not a pursuer of dishonest gain
1 Timothy 3:8; Titus 1:7

Relation to Self

Disciplined
Titus 1:8

Temperate
1 Timothy 3:2, 8; Titus 1:7

Not a lover of money
1 Timothy 3:3

Self-controlled
1 Timothy 3:2; Titus 1:8

Not quick-tempered
Titus 1:7

Not given to drunkenness
1 Timothy 3:3, 8; Titus 1:7

Relation to Family

Having one wife
1 Timothy 3:2, 12

Managing family well
1 Timothy 3:4, 12; Titus 1:6

Having obedient children
1 Timothy 3:4-5, 12; Titus 1:6

Subject

- Greek Word: *presbyteros*; literally "an older person"
- In ancient days the aged were rulers. Term developed into title given to any ruler, of any age.
- N.T. use: generally of ruling office: elders of Jewish nation (Acts 4:8), elders of Christian church (Acts 14:23)
- Church eldership not from Jewish eldership

Qualification of Elder
1 Timothy 3:1-7 / Titus 1:5-9

- A blameless life (righteous behavior, Titus 1:6-8; 1 Timothy 3:2,9)
- Holds to the word (faithful to doctrine, Titus 1:9)
- Even-tempered (not a fighter; patient, 1 Tim. 3:3; Titus 1:7-8)
- Able to teach (assumes knowledge, 1 Tim. 3:2)
- A lover of good (not addicted to wine, greedy for money, unfair, selfish, 1 Tim. 3:3; Titus 1:8)
- A sober, sound mind (thinking through problems, 1 Tim. 3:2; Titus 1:7)
- A family man having one wife and faithful children (1 Tim. 3:2,4; Titus 1:6)
- A mature Christian (only mature can handle authority of leadership, 1 Tim. 3:6)
- A good reputation with those outside church godly out = godly in (1 Tim. 3:7)
- Must be a man (women not permitted to rule in the church, 1 Timothy 2:11-12)

Duties of Elder

- Administrative (to rule the church as a steward of God, Titus 1:7; 1 Pet. 5:2-3)
- Pastoral (to shepherd the church feed the church flock, Acts 20:28; 1 Pet. 5:2)
- Educational (to teach the church correction, exhortation, 1 Tim. 3:2; Titus 1:9)
- Officiative (to lead the church to preside over the church, James 5:14)
- Representative (to represent the church when necessary, Acts 20:17-31)

Authority of Elder

- The authority of the elder is spiritual; his authority is not ecclesiastical—that is, it is not foundational to the existence or continuation of the church.
- The authority of the elder is delegated by the church. The elder has no authority in the church other than that given him by the church. It is given by the church and can be taken from him by the church.
- The elder's authority is limited to the local church that elected him.

Number of Elders

- Plurality of elders was common in each of the early New Testament churches (Acts 14:23; 20:17; Phil. 1:1; Titus 1:5).
- 1 Timothy 3:2 is an example of singular eldership: "bishop;" but this is most likely referring to a leader, a president of the elders/deacons.
- No definite number is laid down for the church to elect.
- Plural eldership with apparent equal authority (James 5:14)

Election of Elder

- One who seeks this office seeks a "noble task" (1 Tim. 3:1).
- The church needs to conduct a careful investigation to see if a man's life lines up with the qualifications (1 Tim. 3:1-13; Titus 1:5-9).
- Length of eldership is unspecified.

Ordination of Elder

- "Ordination": should refer to an act of "appointing," not to formal ceremony of induction into office.
- Ordination ceremony is as follows: laying on of hands, prayer, fasting, a reading of qualifications, vows.
- The elders of the church should be in charge of the ceremony, as they should be of all official meetings.
- Ordination is the church's recognition of the spiritual fitness in its chosen officers. Acts 6:3-6

Dignity of Elder

- Jesus was called "bishop" (1 Pet. 2:25). Peter was named a "fellow-elder" (1 Pet. 5:1). John was an elder (2 John 1). The church was exhorted to respect the dignity of this office (1 Thess. 5:12-13; Heb. 13:7, 17, 24).

Responsibility of Elder

- The elder is to be seen and to see himself as a steward of God (1 Cor. 4:1-2; Titus 1:7).

Rewards of Elder

- He will have increases in authority (Luke 12:43-44). He will also have an eternal crown of glory that is not (1 Pet. 5:1-4) for all Christians but for the faithful elder.

78. The Office of Deacon

Subject	Components / Support / Scripture			
Office of Deacon	*Diakonos* (deacon) Means one who serves.	New Testament use of *diakonos* (διάκονος): as "minister," 20 times (e.g., Eph. 3:7); "servant," 7 times (Matt. 23:11; John 2:5); "deacon" 3 times (Phil. 1:1; 1 Tim. 3:8, 12). *	Term is applied to special office of service in church.	Possible origin: the seven servants of Act 6:1-6.
Qualifications of Deacons 1 Timothy 3	Character: 1 Timothy 3:8 Grace, not double tongued not given to much wine, not greedy for money, able to handle funds for poor. Must handle money matters well in general for church.	Faith: 1 Timothy 3:9 Must hold the mysteries of faith in pure conscience. Does not have to have gift or natural ability for teaching but must understand and hold doctrine.	Family Relations: 1 Timothy 3:12 Same expectation that the elder must meet. Must be husband of one wife, ruling children well. This brings trust to church as deacon handles church affairs.	
	Reputation: Acts 6:3 Known to be full of the Holy Spirit and of wisdom.	Judgment: 1 Timothy 3:2-4 A person of good judgment. Sensible, sober, self-controlled.	Spirituality: Acts 6:3 Full of the Spirit. Handing the funds for the poor and serving tables requires more than business skill and worldly wisdom.	Sex: 1 Timothy 3:11 Women are eligible for this office. They have special qualifications. Must not slander or gossip because much of their service includes visitation. See Romans 16:1—Phoebe. Another view is that the passage refers to wives of deacons instead of deaconesses.
Duties of Deacon	To help the poor. Work of the local church is to help its own poor. Acts 6:1-6 and 1 Timothy 3:8 suggest deacons are to handle church funds.		Relieve elders. This pertains to a number of ministries that allow the elders to continue their spiritual emphasis in the church.	
Election of Deacons	A time of probation is needed (1 Tim. 3:10).	Formal election is carried out by the church (Acts 6:1-6).	The number of deacons was always plural in the early church. (Acts 6:1-6; Phil. 1:1).	
Term of Deacons	Length of term is not specified.			
Dignity of Deacons	The very term implies much honor.	Angelic service (Matt. 4:11), like that of the Lord himself (Matt. 20:28)		
Rewards of Deacons	Good reputation, respect (1 Tim. 3:7-8), wisdom and boldness (Acts 6:8-10)			

*Usage may vary according to translation of Bible that is used.

79. Four Views on Water Baptism

View	Roman Catholic Means of saving grace	Lutheran Imparting saving grace on the one exercising true faith
Statement of View/Meaning of Baptism	"By either awakening or strengthening faith, baptism effects the washing of regeneration." For Catholics this occurs with baptism *ex opere operato*, or by the working of the element itself. Faith does not have to be present. The work is solely God's work in the person. Eradicates both original sin and venial sins. Infuses sanctifying grace.	In order for baptism to be effectual, saving faith must be exercised prior to the baptism. Without saving grace baptism is ineffectual.
Subject	Infants and adults	Adults and children
Mode	Sprinkling	Sprinkling or immersion
Support	Acts 22:16 and Titus 3:5 link salvation and baptism together. Acts 2:38 links repentance and baptism for salvation. Other scriptural support: John 3:5; Romans 6:3; 1 Corinthians 6:11; 1 John 3:9; 5:8 Church father support: Barnabas letter, Pastor Hermas, St. Justin, Tertullian, Cyprian. Council of Trent supported view.	Acts 2:41; 8:36-38; 10:47-48; 16:15,31-34; 18:8; Romans 6:1-11
Objections	Ephesians 2:8-9 says salvation is by grace through faith. New Testament emphasis is on faith apart from works. Baptism linked closely to conversion in New Testament, but never a requirement for conversion. New Testament believers were all adults. No clear example of infant baptism in New Testament.	This position differs from the Catholic view only with respect to faith. The Catholic view does not require saving faith on the part of one being baptized. The baptism is effectual in and of itself. Mark 16:16 does not reflect the need for baptism. In Mark 16:16 only unbelief condemns. The use of baptism as a means of securing grace is not clearly taught by Christ or Paul. This suggests that it is not essential. The many people Jesus dealt with were not confronted with baptismal needs, but only with the need for faith. To incorporate baptism with faith for salvation violates Ephesians 2:8-9. The problem of works exists.

79. Four Views on Water Baptism (continued)

View	Reformed Sign and seal of the covenant	Baptist Token of salvation
Statement of View/Meaning of Baptism	The sacraments are outward signs and seals of an inward reality. "Baptism is the act of faith by which we are brought into the covenant and hence experience its benefits." Baptism is the initiation into the covenant and a sign of salvation.	It is simply a testimony—the first profession of faith that the believer makes. The rite shows the community that the individual is now identified with Christ. It is a symbol of an inward reality and is not sacrament. There is no objective effect upon the person.
Subject	Infants and adults	Believing adults and believing children
Mode	Sprinkling or pouring	Immersion
Support	Baptism continues the covenant made with Abraham and his seed (Gen. 17:7). Baptism replaces circumcision (Acts 2:39; Rom. 4:13-18; Gal. 3:13-18; Heb. 6:13-18; Col. 2:11-12). Whole families included in baptism just as in the Old Testament families were included in the covenant (Acts 16:15, 33; 18:19).	In New Testament, saving faith is always prerequisite to salvation. New Testament examples show adult believers being baptized. Baptism by immersion best pictures the death of Christ and his resurrection. Many New Testament texts discuss salvation by faith apart from baptism (Luke 23:43; Acts 16:30-31; Eph. 2:8-9).
Objections	Church and Israel are not the same entity. Circumcision marked entrance into theocracy which included both believers and unbelievers. Circumcision was for males only; baptism is for all believers. New Testament believers were all adults. No clear example of infant baptism in New Testament.	New Testament has examples of household baptism, which probably included children (Acts 16:29-34). Early church apparently baptized unbelieving infants of believing parents. Many New Testament verses closely link baptism and salvation.

80. Four Views on the Lord's Supper

	Transubstantiation	Consubstantiation	Reformed	Memorial
Groups (Denominations)	Roman Catholic	Lutheran	Presbyterian, other Reformed Churches	Baptist, Mennonite
"Founder" of position	Thomas Aquinas	Martin Luther	John Calvin	Ulrich Zwingli
Presence of Christ	Through consecration of the bread and the wine, the bread changes into Christ's body and wine changes into Christ's blood. Christ is truly and substantially present in the elements themselves.	The elements do not change into the presence of Christ, but he is actually present in, with, and under the elements.	Christ is not literally present in the elements. He is present spiritually in the partaking of the elements.	Christ is not present in the elements either literally or spiritually.
Significance of Lord's Supper	Spiritual food for the soul; it strengthens participant and frees from venial sins. Christ is sacrificed at each Mass to atone for the sins of the partaker.	Recipient has the forgiveness of his sins and the confirmation of his faith. Participation must include faith or the sacrament conveys no benefit.	A commemoration of Christ's death that bestows grace to seal partakers in the love of Christ. The supper gives spiritual nourishment and brings one closer to the presence of Christ.	A commemoration of the death of Christ. The partaker is reminded of the benefits of redemption and salvation brought about in Christ's death.

80. Four Views on the Lord's Supper (continued)

	Transubstantiation	Consubstantiation	Reformed	Memorial
Major Documents	Decrees of Council of Trent	Augsburg Confession Smaller Catechism	Westminster Confession Second Helvetic Confession	Schleithem Confession Dordrecht Confession
Proper Administrator	Priest	Ordained Minister	Pastor Church Leaders	Pastor Church Leaders
Participants	Bread to church members. Cup is withheld from the laity	Believers only	Believers only	Believers only (Some groups practice close communion, where participant must be a member of denomination. Others practice closed communion, where one must be member of local church assembly).
Interpretation of "This is my Body"	Literal Interpretation	Literal Interpretation	Nonliteral Interpretation	Nonliteral Interpretation
Points of Agreement	1. The Lord's Supper was established by Jesus himself (Matt. 26:26-28; Mark 14:22-24; Luke 22:19-20). 2. Jesus commanded the repetition of the Lord's Supper (Matt. 26:29). 3. The Lord's Supper proclaims the death of Jesus Christ (I Cor. 11:26). 4. The Lord's Supper imparts some type of spiritual benefit to the participant.			

81. Church Discipline

"Many people fail to make a clear distinction between punishment and discipline, and there is a very significant difference between these two concepts. *Punishment* is designed to execute *retribution* for a wrong done. *Discipline*, on the other hand, is to encourage the *restoration* of one involved in wrongdoing. Punishment is designed primarily to avenge a wrong and assert justice. Discipline is designed primarily as a corrective for the one who has failed to live according to the standards of the church and/or society."*

Passage	Problem	Procedure	Purpose
Matthew 18:15-18	The sin of a "brother" (undefined)	1. Private reproof 2. Private conference 3. Public announcement 4. Public exclusion	Restoration (to win "your brother over")
1 Corinthians 5	Immorality Greed Idolatry Drunkenness Swindling	1. Corporate grief 2. Removal from midst 3. No association	Restoration (5:5) Purification (5:7)
2 Corinthians 2:5-11	Unnamed	After sincere repentance 1. Forgive him. 2. Comfort him. 3. Love him.	Restoration (2:7) Protection (2:11)
Galatians 6:1	"A sin"	Restore him 1. As spiritual persons 2. With meekness 3. With reflection	Restoration (2:11)
2 Thessalonians 3:6-15	Laziness, gossip ("busy-bodies")	1. Take note of him. 2. Keep aloof from him. 3. Admonish him (as a brother, not an enemy).	Restoration ("He may feel ashamed.")
1 Timothy 5:19-20	An accusation against an elder entertained without witnesses	1. Need 2-3 witnesses. 2. If sin continues, then rebuke before all.	Purification (so "others may take warning")
Titus 3:9-11	Divisiveness	1. Give 2 warnings. 2. Reject him (as warped, sinful, self-condemned).	Protection (against division)

126

*Carl Laney, *A Guide to Church Discipline* (Minneapolis, MN: Bethany, 1985), p. 79.

82. Church Discipline Flowchart

1. Open sexual immorality (1 Corinthians 5:1–13)

2. Unresolved personal conflicts (Matthew 18:15–20)

3. Divisiveness (Romans 16:17–18; Titus 3:10)

4. False teaching (Galatians 1:8, 9; 1 Timothy 1:20; 6:3–5; 2 John 9–11; Revelation 2:14-16)

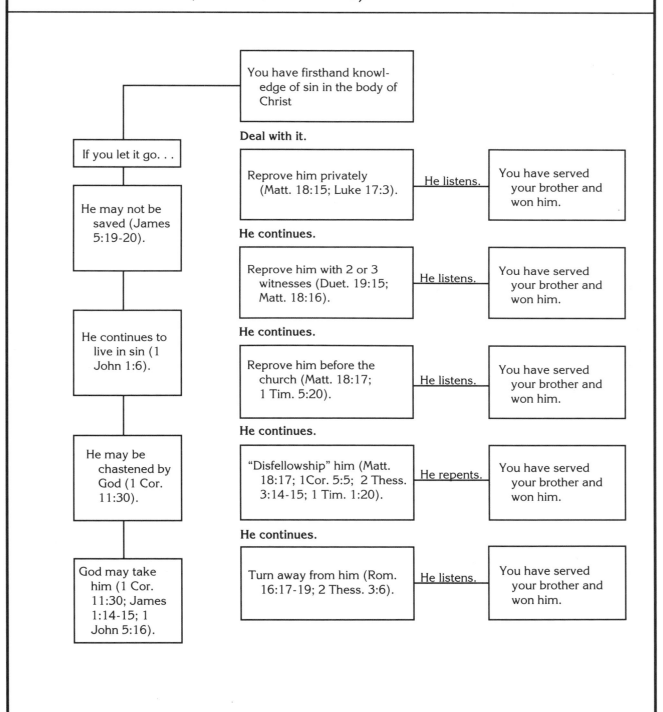

You have firsthand knowledge of sin in the body of Christ

If you let it go. . .

He may not be saved (James 5:19-20).

He continues to live in sin (1 John 1:6).

He may be chastened by God (1 Cor. 11:30).

God may take him (1 Cor. 11:30; James 1:14-15; 1 John 5:16).

Deal with it.

Reprove him privately (Matt. 18:15; Luke 17:3). — He listens. — You have served your brother and won him.

He continues.

Reprove him with 2 or 3 witnesses (Duet. 19:15; Matt. 18:16). — He listens. — You have served your brother and won him.

He continues.

Reprove him before the church (Matt. 18:17; 1 Tim. 5:20). — He listens. — You have served your brother and won him.

He continues.

"Disfellowship" him (Matt. 18:17; 1Cor. 5:5; 2 Thess. 3:14-15; 1 Tim. 1:20). — He repents. — You have served your brother and won him.

He continues.

Turn away from him (Rom. 16:17-19; 2 Thess. 3:6). — He listens. — You have served your brother and won him.

83. Key Terms to the Second Coming of Christ

Terms	"Parousia"	"Apocalypse"	"Epiphany"
Scripture References	1 Thessalonians 3:13 1 Thessalonians 4:15	1 Corinthians 1:7 2 Thessalonians 1:6-7 1 Peter 4:13	1 Timothy 6:14 2 Timothy 4:8 Titus 2:13–14
Literal Meaning	"being by" "presence"	"revelation"	"appearance"
Translated Meaning	"presence" "coming" "arrival"	"to reveal"	"to appear"

84. Views on the Rapture

Pretribulation

Statement of View	Stated: Christ will come for his saints; afterward he will come with his saints. The first stage of Christ's coming is called the Rapture; the second is called the revelation. The older school emphasized the issue of "imminency." However, in recent days the crux of this position centers more around the aspect of God's wrath and whether the church is called to experience any or all of it during the Tribulation.
Proponents	John F. Walvoord, J. Dwight Pentecost, John Feinberg, Paul Feinberg, Herman Hoyt, Charles Ryrie, Rene Pache, Henry C. Thiessen, Leon Wood, Hal Lindsey, Alva McClain, John A. Sproul, Richard Mayhue.

Arguments For	Arguments Against
The Bible says that Christians (the church) are exempt from divine wrath (1 Thess. 1:10). This exemption does not mean that the church does not experience trials, persecution, or suffering.	Christians are exempt from God's wrath ($\dot{o}\rho\gamma\eta$), but the majority of passages dealing with tribulation ($\theta\lambda\iota\psi\iota\varsigma$) refer to the tribulation that believers suffer. Exemption from wrath does not mean exemption from tribulation. Also, if Christians are exempt from wrath of the Tribulation, those who believe during the Tribulation would need to be raptured at conversion.
The believers are also exempt from the time of wrath recorded in Revelation 3:10. This is supported by the way the Greek preposition *ek* ($\dot{e}\kappa$) is used in this passage.	Normative meaning of *ek* ($\dot{e}\kappa$) is "out from the midst of" and does not require a snatching from trial. It can mean kept form tribulation without being taken from trial. The normal preposition for "keeping away from" is $\dot{a}\pi o$.
All positions of tribulation rapture predict a millennial kingdom. The pre-tribulation position calls for living, nonglorified believers to enter the kingdom, thus to repopulate the kingdom (Zech. 12:10-13:1; Rom. 11:26).	144,000 of Revelation can populate the Earth during the time of the Millennium.
This position offers a clear distinction between the Rapture and the revelation, an interval of time. This is consistent with various Scriptures that discuss both these events. For the Rapture: John 14:1-14; 1 Cor. 15:51-58; 1 Thess. 4:13-18; for the revelation, or the second coming of Christ: Zech. 14; Matt. 24:29-31; Mark 13:24-27; Luke 21:25-27; Rev. 19.	The "blessed hope" and "glorious appearing" are the same events (Rapture and revelation). The New Testament speaks of one second coming, not of two comings or of a coming in two stages. The distinction may be in the nature of events not in time differences.
This position stresses imminency. Christ can return at any time; therefore believers have an attitude of expectancy (Titus 2:13). There are no preparatory warnings of an impending tribulation for the church–age believers (Acts 20:29-30; 2 Peter 2:1; 1 John 4:1-3).	Imminency for the apostles and the early church during this time revolved around the second coming of Christ. Thus, the two events are coterminous, not separate (Matt. 24:3, 27, 37, 39; 2 Thess. 2:8; James 5:7-8; 1 John 2:28). Also, 2 Thessalonians 2:1-10 may list events to be expected before the Rapture.
This position sees a literal Tribulation as given in Revelation 6-19. These is no mentioned of the church (argument from silence) in Revelation 4-18.	Much language in Revelation 6-19 is figurative, the tribulation may be as well. Argument from silence is inherently weak reasoning.
The Restrainer mentioned in 2 Thessalonians 2:1-12 is the Holy Spirit indwelling the church. He must remove her (the church) before the Tribulation begins.	Holy Spirit's indwelling ministry is not equivalent to his restraining work. Also, passage does not clearly equate the restrainer with the Holy Spirit, or the removal of the restraint with a rapture of the church.

129

Several portions of this chart from adapted from Millard J. Erickson, *Christian Theology* Vol. 3 (Grand Rapids: Baker Book House, 1985), pp. 1149-1224. Used by permission; also Gleason L. Archer, Jr., Paul D. Feinberg, Douglas J. Moo, and Richard R. Reiter, *The Rapture: Pre-, Mid-, Post-Tribulational?* (Grand Rapids: Zondervan, 1984). Used by permission.

84. Views on the Rapture (continued)

Partial Rapture

Statement of View	This position states that only believers who are watching and waiting for the Lord will be raptured at various times before and during the seven–year Tribulation. Those who are raptured are spiritually mature saints, both dead and living (1 Thess. 4:13-18).
Proponents	Joseph Seiss, G. H. Lang, Robert Govett, Witness Lee, G. H. Pember, Ira E. David, D. H. Panton

Arguments For	Arguments Against
New Testament often views the resurrection as a reward to be strived for (Matt. 19:28-29; Luke 9:62; 20:35; Phil. 3:10-14; Rev. 2;11; 3:5). Therefore, not all believers will gain the first resurrection, only those who are worthy.	Rapture is part of the culmination of salvation. God starts salvation by grace and will finish it by his grace, not by our works. (Eph. 2:8-9)
Other Scriptures indicate partial rapture of believers, or an idea similar to this (Matt. 24:40-51).	There is confusion between verses that apply to Israel and verses that apply to the church in the Gospel passages. This is not the Rapture, but a taking away to judgment as in the example of the Flood in Matthew 24:39. 1 Corinthians 15:51-52 says all believers will be raptured.
There is an emphasis on watching, waiting, working, and the hope of rewards (Matt. 24:41-42; 25:1-13; 1 Thess. 5:6; Heb. 9:28).	The emphasis is on working for rewards (crowns, 2 Tim. 4:8) not for participation in the Rapture.
There are verses that emphasize the need to suffer in order to reign (Rom. 8:16-17; Luke 22:28-30; Acts 14:22; Col. 3:24; 2 Thess. 1:4-5). Therefore, believers must suffer now or during the Tribulation before they can reign with Christ.	Believers suffer in every age, and all believers will reign with Christ. The suffering and reigning of Christians is never linked to any supposed order of the rapture.
A believer, through sinning, can lose his right to enjoy the first resurrection and the kingdom (1 Cor. 6:19-20; Gal. 5:19-21; Heb. 12:14).	These passages speak of the unsaved not entering the kingdom. They do not apply to believers.
Worthy, watching believers will be rewarded by being raptured before the Tribulation (Rev. 3:10).	There is the division in the church, the body of Christ. It seems that those worthy of being translated will be raptured, while those not worthy will be left behind. Passages like John 14:1; I Corinthians 15:51-52 obviously include all believers.
Since the baptism of the Spirit empowers to witness (Acts 1:8) and not all believers witness, not all believers are in the body of Christ (1 Cor. 12: 13) and not all are raptured.	The baptism of the Spirit places all believers in the body of Christ (1 Cor. 12:13).

Midtribulation

Statement of View	This position sees that the church, believers in Christ, are raptured in the middle of the tribulation period, prior to the Great Tribulation. This view offers the best of the pretribulation and posttribulation positions. It also has the mid-seventieth-week Rapture.
Proponents	Gleason L. Archer, Norman Harrison, J. Oliver Buswell, Merrill C. Tenney, G. H. Lang

Arguments For	Arguments Against
This position offers fewer problems than either the pre- or posttribulational views. It avoids the problems of the two extremes.	There is a loss of imminency in this position (as also in posttribulation). No longer are we called upon to wait and watch, but to look for preparatory signs, as given in the book of Revelation and in Matthew 24:1-14.
There is a great emphasis on the 3 1/2 years (42 months, 1,260 days) in the Scripture to divide the 7 years of Tribulation (Dan. 7; 9:27; 12:7; Rev. 11:23; 12:3 , 6, 14).	The emphasis on the middle of the Tribulation is due to the breaking of the covenant with Israel (Dan. 9:27), not because of the Rapture.
The Olivet Discourse (Matt. 24-25) talks of the coming, appearing, and return of Christ. It coincides with the Rapture passage in 1 Thessalonians 4:15.	The only concrete link is the use of *parousia* in both passages. Many other differences in the contexts make this a weak link.
2 Thessalonians 2:14 clearly specifies preceding signs to the Rapture.	2 Thessalonians 2:1ff. refers to the two events preceding the Day of the Lord, not the rapture of the church.
Revelation 11:15-19 mentions the seventh trumpet, which is identical to the trumpet of God in 1 Thessalonians 4:16.	Does the Rapture truly occur in Revelation 11 just because there is a trumpet sound? The argument is weak and has no biblical basis.
This position keeps the distinction between the Rapture and revelation, thus two stages in the coming of Christ.	Pretribulation also maintains temporal distinction. Posttribulation maintains a distinction as well, though it is a difference in essence rather than time.
The church is delivered from the wrath of God but not from trials and testing, since the Rapture occurs in the middle of the Tribulation, just prior to the great outpouring of God's wrath.	Those who hold this view must devise a new concept of wrath in the book of Revelation. There is forced spiritualization of chapters 1-11 for contemporary purposes and not future fulfillment. The church can be delivered from wrath either by pretribulation rapture or by protection from wrath.
Just as there is overlapping in the book of Acts in terms of the program of God for the church and Israel, so there is overlapping in the program of God in the book of Revelation.	The church has both Jews and Gentiles in it. This does not necessitate, however, an overlapping of God's program for the church and for national Israel.
This view allows for the nonglorified saints at the end of the Tribulation to enter the millennial kingdom to repopulate the world.	Pretribulation also allows for repopulation. Also, it is possible that some unbelievers will enter the Millennium since the conversion of Israel will not take place until the Second Advent.

84. Views on the Rapture (continued)

Posttribulation

Statement of View	This position asserts that the living believers are to be raptured at the second coming of Christ, which will occur at the end of the Tribulation. Within this camp, there are four views as categorized by Walvoord: (a) classic, (b) semiclassic, (c) futurist, (d) dispensational. The spectrum is broad, encompassing a period of time from the early church fathers to the present century.
Proponents	Classic: J. Barton Payne Semiclassic: Alexander Reese, Norman MacPherson, George L. Rose, George H. Fromow Futurist: George Ladd, Dave MacPherson Dispensational: Robert H. Gundry, Douglas J. Moo Others: Harold Ockenga, J. Sidlow Baxter

Arguments For	Arguments Against
The Rapture is preceded by unmistakable signs (Matt. 24:3-31). These signs are part of the tribulation period the saints must go through. The culmination will be the return of Christ, which involves the rapture of believers (Matt. 24:29-31, 40-41). In the Olivet Discourse Christ does talk of the Rapture with the revelation.	The position raises problems about the repopulation of the millennial kingdom by flesh and blood believers if they are all raptured and glorified.
The parable of the wheat and tares (Matt. 13:24) shows that separation takes place at the end of the age. At that time, the good (believers) are distinguished from the bad (unbelievers), and this occurs at the end of the Tribulation.	The view that the 144,000 in Revelation are the ones who populate the earth fails to take the context of this passage into consideration.
The order of resurrection demands that all believers of all ages be brought back in their glorified bodies at the end of the Tribulation (Rev. 20:4-6).	Their exegetical argument of Revelation 3:10 with *ek* ("from") is weak. To interpret "trial" as anything else but God's wrath is not doing justice to this word or the text.
The New Testament words on the return of Christ make no distinction of stages: epiphany, manifestation, revelation, parousia, the day, that day, the day of Jesus Christ, the day of the Lord Jesus, and the day of the Lord.	The sequence of events, connecting 1 Thessalonians 4 with the Rapture and 1 Thessalonians 5 with the Day of the Lord, is glossed over in determining chronological order of events.
The phrase "keep you from the hour of trial" in Revelation 3:10 can also refer to deliverance from the wrath of Satan as it operates in the Tribulation period.	Just as Scripture may be somewhat silent regarding a pretribulation rapture, so there is greater silence in a posttribulation rapture. This is especially true in John's prophetic letter of Revelation, where there is more emphasis on the return of Christ. A case in point is the vague mention of the church in Revelation 4-18.
The rise in apostasy is a sign that will precede the return of Christ (2 Thess. 2:8).	The argument that a posttribulation rapture was the belief of the historic Christian church falls apart when we see that what was believed in the early church is quite different from what is believed today. Nevertheless, the basis of a doctrinal truth is not the early church, but the Word of God.
Much of scriptural teaching to the church concerning the end times is meaningless if the church does not go through the Tribulation (Matt. 24:15-20).	This position conflicts with the teaching of the imminent return of Christ. Scripture teaches us to wait and watch, not for preparatory signs of Christ's coming but for the blessed hope of his return (Titus 2:13).

85. Views on the Millennium

<table>
<tr>
<td colspan="2">

Historic Premillennialism
(Also called Classical and Nondispensational Premillennialism)

</td>
</tr>
<tr>
<td>

Statement of View

</td>
<td>

Premillennialists hold that the return of Christ will be preceded by certain signs, then followed by a period of peace and righteousness in which Christ will reign on earth in person as King. Historic premillennialists understand the return of Christ and the Rapture as one and the same event. They see unity. Therefore they stand apart from the dispensational premillennialist who sees these as two events separated by the seven-year Tribulation. Premillennialism was the dominant eschatological interpretation in the first three centuries of the Christian church. Early fathers Papias, Irenaeus, Justin Martyr, Tertullian, and others held to this view.

</td>
</tr>
<tr>
<td>

Proponents

</td>
<td>

George E. Ladd, J. Barton Payne, Alexander Reese, Millard Erickson

</td>
</tr>
</table>

Arguments for	Arguments Against
The chronology of Revelation 10-20 shows that immediately following the second coming of Christ the following will occur: the binding of Satan (20:1-3), the first resurrection (20:4-6), and the beginning of the reign of Christ (20:4-7) for a "thousand years." (17-18)*	The reign of Christ does not begin after the first resurrection for he now reigns at the right hand of the Father (Heb. 1:3). (178-79)
At the present time, the church is the spiritual Israel. God will return the nation of Israel to her rightful place to fulfill the promises of the kingdom (Rom. 11) in the millennial kingdom. This passage supports the teaching of verse 24: "How much more readily will these, who are the natural branches be grafted into their own olive tree?" (18-29)	While the church benefits spiritually from the promises made to Israel, Israel and the church are never specifically equated. (42-44) A kingdom composed of both glorified saints and people still in the flesh seems too unreal to be possible. (49)
The Old Testament and Christ predicted a kingdom in which the Anointed One would rule (Ps. 2 ; Matt. 25:24).	The kingdom is an overall teaching of the Bible. It now lies in the church (Matt. 12:28; Luke 17:20-21). Christ reigns now in heaven (Heb. 1:3; 2:7-8). (178-79)
As the prophecies of the Old Testament were fulfilled in the past, so those concerning the future will be too. This is an argument for consistency in hermeneutics. (27-29)	The interpretation of Revelation 20:1-7 does not necessitate literalism. These verses can be understood symbolically, since the book of Revelation employs many symbols. (161)
The church serves to fulfill some of the promises made to Israel. Christ made this clear after the Jews rejected him (Matt. 12:28; Luke 17:20-21). (20-26)	This view insists that the New Testament interprets the Old Testament prophecies in cases where the New Testament actually is applying a principle found in an Old Testament prophecy (Hos. 11:1 in Matt. 2:15; Hos. 1:10 & 2:23 in Rom. 9:24-26). (42-43) The understanding of "came to life" (Rev. 20:4) can be understood to mean "living," and not resurrection.
Many of the early church fathers held to this view of eschatology. (9)	It is not easy to place the church fathers definitely into one view of eschatology. Also, doctrine is not determined by a survey of church fathers, but by study of Scripture. (41)
A literal 1000-year earthly reign is referred to in only one passage (Rev. 20:1-6) and it is mentioned in apocalyptic literature. The Old Testament cannot be used to supply material on the Millennium. (32)	The Old Testament prophecies provide the basis for New Testament prophecies. The New Testament sets the place and duration of the Millennium (Rev. 20:1-6), and the Old Testament gives much of the nature of the Millennium. (43-46)
Romans 11:26 says that national Israel will be converted. (27-28)	Many passages in the New Testament dissolve distinctions between Israel and the church (Gal. 2;28-29; 3;7; Eph 2:14-16). (109)
God has made a special place for national Israel in his program. (27-28)	Israel was chosen as a nation through which the Messiah would come. Since Jesus finished his work, Israel's unique purpose has been fulfilled. (53)

*The numbers following each of the statements refers to pages in Robert G. Clouse, *The Meaning of the Millennium: Four Views* (Downers Grove: InterVarsity Press, 1977). Used by permission. Other statements are from a variety of writers.

85. Views on the Millennium (continued)

Dispensational Premillennialism

Statement of View	Adherents of this school are represented by those who generally hold to the concept of two-stages in the coming of Christ. He will come *for* his church (Rapture) and then *with* his church (revelation). The two events are separated by a seven-year Tribulation. There is a consistent distinction between Israel and the church throughout history.
Proponents	J. N. Darby, C. I. Scofield, Lewis Sperry Chafer, John Walvoord, Charles Feinberg, Herman Hoyt, Harry Ironside, Alva McClain, Eric Sauer, Charles Ryrie

Arguments For	Arguments Against
This view maintains a consistent hermeneutic that allows Israel to fulfill promises given to them and the church to fulfill its promise. (66-68)	Israel fulfilled its land promises once in the conquest (Josh. 21:43, 45). Its purpose of bringing forth the Messiah has also been fulfilled. (101)
The "coming to life" (Rev. 20:4-5) being designated as the first resurrection supports this view. This resurrection precedes the millennial reign. (37-38)	This resurrection is not a bodily-resurrection because only one bodily resurrection occurs (John 5:28-29; Acts 24:15). This is a spiritual resurrection. (56-58; 168)
Scriptures reveal both a universal and a mediatorial kingdom which are two aspects of God's rule. The mediatorial kingdom is the Millennium, in which Christ will reign on earth. (72-73ff; 91)	God's rule over the creation has always been through a mediator. Thus his mediatorial rule cannot be restricted to the Millennium. (93)
A literal reading of Revelation 19-20 leads to a dispensational premillennial view. Other views must spiritualize the events.	Much of Revelation must be understood symbolically because of its apocalyptic nature.
The Abrahamic covenant will be completely fulfilled in Israel (Gen. 12:1-3). Its outworking is seen in the Palestinian, Davidic, and new covenants. The church shares the blessings of the new covenant, but does not fulfill its promises (Gal. 3:16).	The promises made to Old Testament Israel were always conditional, based on Israel's obedience and faithfulness. The new covenant is for the church, not for Israel. (100)
The concept of a literal earthly kingdom is an outgrowth of the overall kingdom teachings in both Old and New Testaments. (42-43)	The New Testament, which is the sole authority for the church, replaced the Old Testament and its promises. (97)
The Millennium is possible and necessary because not all of the promises given to Israel have been fulfilled. (Enns, 390)	Israel's disobedience negated their promises, which were based on their faithfulness (Jer. 18:9-10). (98)
The Old Testament describes the kingdom as a literal on-earth reign of Messiah over the whole world. (79-84)	The New Testament shows that Christ established a kingdom at his first coming and is now reigning over the whole world. (102)

85. Views on the Millennium (continued)

Postmillennialism

Statement of View	Postmillennialists believe that the kingdom of God is now extended through teaching, preaching, evangelization, and missionary activities. The world is to be Christianized, and the result will be a long period of peace and prosperity called the Millennium. This will be followed by Christ's return. This position is seemingly gaining more adherents in contemporary circles, such as the Christian Reconstruction Institute for Christian Studies. The leading proponent of traditional postmillennium was Loraine Boettner. See his book *The Millennium* (Philadelphia: Presbyterian and Reformed Publishing Co., 1957).
Proponents	Augustine, Loraine Boettner, A. Hodge, Charles Hodge, W. G. T. Shedd, A. H. Strong, B. B. Warfield, Joachim of Fiore, Daniel Whitby, James Snowden, Christian Reconstructionists

Arguments For	Arguments Against
The rule of the Spirit of God in the heart of the believer is in one sense a millennium (John 14-16). (121)	This view fails to deal adequately with Revelation 20 in formulating and defining its concept of the Millennium. (Erickson, 1208)
The universal diffusion of the gospel is promised by Christ (Matt. 28:18-20).	The Great Commission does command universal gospel proclamation, but the world is characterized by spiritual decline, not spiritual growth.
Christ's throne is in heaven where he is now reigning and ruling (Ps. 47:2; 97:5). The church has the job of proclaiming that truth and seeing people come to faith in him. (118-119)	Neither of these statements necessitates postmillennialism or preclude a future earthly reign.
Salvation will come to all nations, tribes, peoples, and tongues (Rev. 7:9-10).	While salvation will come to all nations, this does not mean that all, or nearly all, will be saved. Nor does the New Testament say the Gospel is designed to improve the social conditions in the world.
Christ's parable of the mustard seed shows how the gospel extends and expands slowly but surely until it covers the whole world (Matt. 13:31-32). The saved will far outnumber the lost in the world. (150-51)	A majority of saved people on earth does not guarantee the golden age that postmillennialism expects to come.
Many evidences exist that show that where the gospel is preached, social and moral conditions are being greatly improved.	The attitude of idealistic optimism overlooks the passages that reveal the distress and apostasy of the end times (Matt. 24:3-14; 1 Tim. 4:1-5; 2 Tim. 3:1-7). Also, just as many evidences can be gathered to prove that the world conditions are declining. (151)
Through the preaching of the gospel and the saving work of the Spirit, the world will be Christianized and Christ will return at the end of a long period of peace commonly called the Millennium. (118)	The use of an allegorical approach to the interpretation of Scripture in Revelation 20 is completely allegorizing the thousand year reign. There is a limited amount of scriptural support for this position.

85. Views on the Millennium (continued)

Amillennialism

Statement of View	The Bible predicts a continuous parallel growth of good and evil in the world between the first coming of Christ and the second coming of Christ. The kingdom of God is now present in the world through his Word, his Spirit, his church. This position has also been called "realized millennialism."
Proponents	Oswald Allis, Louis Berkhof, G. Berkouwer, William Hendriksen, Abraham Kuyper, Leon Morris, Anthony Hoekema, other Reformed theologians, and the Roman Catholic Church.

Arguments for	Arguments Against
The conditional nature of the Abrahamic covenant (as well as the other covenants) indicates that fulfillment of it, or the lack of it, is transferred to the church through Jesus Christ (Gen. 12:1-3; Rom. 10; Gal. 3:16).	Many passages show that the Abrahamic Covenant was unconditional and was to be literally fulfilled by Israel.
The land promises of the Abrahamic covenant were expanded from Jews to all believers and from the land of Canaan to the new earth.	This position has problems in being hermeneutically consistent in the interpretation of the Scriptures. It spiritualizes passages that can clearly be understood literally.
Prophecy demands a symbolic approach to interpreting the Bible. Therefore, prophetic passages can be understood in the overall framework of God's outworking of his covenant (e.g., Rev. 20). (161)	The chronology of Revelation 19-20 is continuous and describes events that will occur in the end of the Tribulation and prior to the thousand- year reign of Christ.
The Old and New Testaments are bound together in unity under the covenant of grace. Israel and the church are not two distinct programs but one unified outworking of God's purposes and plans. (186)	Scripture does not clearly reveal a covenant of grace. This is a theological term coined to fit into the amillennial scheme of eschatology.
The kingdom of God is central in biblical history. It was central in the Old Testament, in Jesus' ministry, and in the church and will consummate with Christ's return. There is no need to call for a kingdom at a latter time, for the kingdom has always been. (177-79)	The position clearly does not see God's having a place for Israel in the future. Amillennialists have difficulty in explaining Romans 11.
History is moving toward the goal of the total redemption of the universe (Eph. 1:10; Col. 1:18). (187)	The total redemption of the universe is the goal of all millennial views. This does not specifically support an amillennial view.
Revelation 20:4-6 refers to the reign of souls with Christ in heaven as he reigns by his word and his spirit. (164-66)	Revelation 20:4-5 clearly refers to a resurrection, yet the amillennialists avoid the issue. Forms of the Greek word zao (ζάω) "to live" are used this way for resurrection in John 5:25 and Revelation 2:8.
The New Testament often equates Israel and the church as a unity (Acts 13:32-39; Gal. 6:15; 1 Peter 2:9). (Hoekema, 197-98)	National Israel and the church are treated as distinct in the New Testament (Acts 3:12; 4:8-10; 21:28; Rom. 9:3-4; 10:1; 11; Eph. 2:12).

86. Dispensational Time Chart of Last Things

Incarnation

Church Age

The ἁρπαγησόμεθα ("catching up")

Interstitial Period

Day of the Lord

Time of Jacob's Trouble (Mid-Tribulation)

The ἀποκαλυψις ("revelation")

The Millennium

Eternal State

Matt. 1:18-23
Gal. 4:4
Phil. 2:6-8

Eph. 2:3-6

1 Thess. 4:17

Mal. 4:5
1 Thess. 5:4
2 Thess. 2:2
2 Pet. 3:10

Dan. 9:27

Matt. 24:30-31
1 Pet. 1:7, 13;
Rev. 1:1

Rev. 20:1-6
Rev. 7:26-27

1 Cor. 15:24-28
Rev. 21-22

87. Views Concerning Last Things

Categories	Amillennialism	Postmillennialism	Historic Premillennialism	Dispensational Premillennialism
Second Coming of Christ	Single event; no distinction between Rapture and Second Coming; introduces eternal state.	Single event; no distinction between Rapture and Second Coming; Christ returns after Millennium.	Rapture and Second Coming simultaneous; Christ returns to reign on earth.	Second Coming in two phases; Rapture of church; second coming to earth 7 years later.
Resurrection	General resurrection of believers and unbelievers at second coming of Christ.	General resurrection of believers and unbelievers at second coming of Christ.	Resurrection of believers at beginning of Millennium. Resurrection of unbelievers at end of Millennium.	Distinction in two resurrections: 1. Church at Rapture; 2. Old Testament/Tribulation saints at Second Coming; 3. Unbelievers at end of Millennium.
Judgments	General judgment of all people.	General judgment of all people.	Judgment at Second Coming. Judgment at end of Tribulation.	Distinction in judgment: 1. Believers' works at Rapture; 2. Jews/Gentiles at end of Tribulation; 3. Unbelievers at end of Millennium.
Tribulation	Tribulation is experienced in this present age.	Tribulation is experienced in this present age.	Posttribulation view: church goes through the future Tribulation.	Pretribulation view: church is raptured prior to Tribulation.
Millennium	No literal Millennium on earth after second coming. Kingdom present in church age.	Present age blends into Millennium because of progress of gospel.	Millennium is both present and future. Christ is reigning in heaven. Millennium not necessarily 1,000 years.	At Second Coming Christ inaugurates literal 1,000-year Millennium on earth.
Israel and the Church	Church is the new Israel. No distinction between Israel and church.	Church is the new Israel. No distinction between Israel and church.	Some distinction between Israel and church. Future for Israel, but church is spiritual Israel.	Complete distinction between Israel and church. Distinct program for each.
Adherents	L. Berkhof; O. T. Allis; G. C. Berkhouwer	Charles Hodge; B. B. Warfield; W. G. T. Shedd; A. H. Strong	G. E. Ladd; A. Reese; M. J. Erickson	L. S. Chafer; J. D. Pentecost; C. C. Ryrie; J. F. Walvoord

Adapted from Paul Enns, *Moody Handbook of Theology* (Chicago: Moody Press, 1989), p. 383. Used by permission.

88. Perspectives on Annihilationism

Statement of View	All people are created immortal, but those continuing in sin are completely annihilated, that is, reduced to nonexistence.
Proponents	Arnobius, Edward Fudge, Clark H. Pinnock, Socinians, John R. W. Stott, B. B. Warfield, John Wenham,
Tenets	There is a literal hell. Not everyone will be saved. There is only one class of future existence. Those who are not saved will be eliminated or annihilated. They will simply cease to exist. No one deserves eternal, conscious suffering.

Arguments For	Arguments Against
That God would allow eternal torment of his creatures is inconsistent with his love.	This view places too much emphasis on the material aspect of man.
Cessation of existence is implied in certain terms applied to the destiny of the wicked, such as destruction (Matt. 7:13; 10:28; 2 Thess. 1:9) and perishing (John 3:16).	There is no lexicographical or exegetical evidence to support the contention that such terms mean annihilation. The way such terms are used in Scripture reveals that they cannot mean annihilaiton.
The eternal punishment spoken of in Matthew 25:46 is just that, not everlasting but eternal.	In Matthew 25:46, the existence of believers and that of unbelievers are set in parallel. Both forms of existence are said to be eternal. The same word is used in both instances. If the passage speaks of everlasting life for the believer, it must also be speaking of everlasting punishment for the unbeliever. Otherwise there are two competing meanings of "eternal" in the same verse.
God alone has immortality (1 Tim. 1:17; 6:16).	God also confers immortality on holy angels and redeemed humanity. God alone has life and immortality in himself (John 5:26), but this does not mean that he has not conferred endless existence as a natural endowment to his rational creatures. Scripture presents death as a punishment for sin (Gen. 2:17; Rom. 5:12) rather than immortality as the reward for obedience.
Imortality is a special gift connected with redemption in Jesus Christ (Rom. 2:7; 1 Cor. 15:52-54; 2 Tim. 1:10).	Eternal life is a quality of life the wicked never experience. The term "eternal life" does not connote unending existence but refers to well-being in true fellowship with God (John 17:3).

89. Eternal Punishment

Description of Eternal Punishment	Darkness (Matt. 8:12) Weeping and gnashing of teeth (Matt. 8:12; 13:50; 22:13; 24:51) Furnace of fire (Matt. 13:50) Eternal fire (Matt. 25:41) Unquenchable fire (Luke 3:17) Bottomless pit (Rev. 9:1-11) Torment forever, no rest day or night (Rev. 14:10-11) Lake of fire (Rev. 19:20; 21:8) Black darkness (Jude 13)
Participants in Eternal Punishment	Satan (Rev. 20:10) The beast and the false prophet (Rev. 20:10) Evil angels (2 Pet. 2:4) Humans (body and soul) are cast into everlasting punishment (Matt. 5:30; 10:28; 18:9; Rev. 20:15)
Effects of Eternal Punishment	Separation from God and his glory (2 Thess. 1:9) Different degrees of punishment (Matt. 11:21-24; Luke 12:47-48) Final eternal state/no second chance (Isa. 66:24; Mark 9:44-48; Matt. 25:46; 2 Thess. 1:9)

Bibliography

Adams, Jay E. *The Time Is at Hand*. Philadelphia: Presbyterian and Reformed, 1970.

Allis, Oswald T. *Prophecy and the Church*. Philadelphia: Presbyterian and Reformed, 1945.

Archer, Jr., Gleason L. "Alleged Errors and Discrepancies in the Original Manuscripts of the Bible," *Inerrancy*, ed. Norman L. Geisler. Grand Rapids: Zondervan, 1979.

Archer, Jr., Gleason L., Paul D. Feinberg, Douglas J. Moo, Richard R. Reiter. *The Rapture: Pre-, Mid-, or Post-Tribulational?* Grand Rapids: Zondervan, 1984.

Augsburger, Myron S. *Quench Not the Spirit*. Scottdale, PA: Herald Press, 1961.

Barrett, C. K. *The Holy Spirit and the Gospel Tradition*. London: Hollen Street Press, 1947.

Belcher, Richard P. *A Comparison of Dispensationalism and Covenant Theology*. Columbia, S. C.: Richbarry Press, 1986.

Berkhof, Louis. *The History of Christian Doctrines*. Grand Rapids: Baker, 1937.

_____. *Systematic Theology*. Grand Rapids: Eerdmans, 1939.

Berkouwer, G.C. *The Person of Christ*. Grand Rapids: Eerdmans, 1954.

Berry, Harold J. "A Sign to Unbelieving Jews," *Good News B* 30:2 (1972):20-22.

Biesner, E. Calvin. *God In Three Persons*. Wheaton: Tyndale, 1984.

Bromiley, G. W. ed. *The International Standard Bible Encyclopedia*.

Brown, Harold O.J. *Heresies*. Gorden City, N.Y.: Doubleday, 1984.

Burns, J. Patout, ed. *Theological Anthropology*. Philadelphia: Fortress Press, 1981.

Calvin, John. *Institute of the Christian Religion*. Trans. Henry Beveridge. Grand Rapids: Eerdmans, 1970.

Carl Brumback. *What Meaneth This?* Springfield, MO: Gospel Publishing House, 1961.

Chafer, Lewis Sperry. *Systematic Theology*. 8 Vols. Dallas: Dallas Seminary Press, 1947, 1948.

_____. *Major Bible Themes*. Grand Rapids: Zondervan, rev. ed., 1974.

Chapman, Colin. *Christianity on Trial*. Wheaton: Tyndale, 1974.

Clouse, Robert G., ed. *The Meaning of the Millennium: Four Views*. Downers Grove, IL.: InterVarsity, 1977.

Cook, W. Robert. "Systematic Theology in Outline Form" unpublished notes from Prolegoema and Bibliology class at Western Seminary: Portland, Oregon: 1981.

Criswell, W.A., ed. *The Criswell Study Bible.* New York: Thomas Nelson, 1979.

Culman, Oscar. *Peter: Disciple, Apostle, and Martyr.* Philadelphia: Westminster Press, 1953.

Delitzsch, Franz J. and Paton J. Gloag. *The Messianic Prophecies of Christ.* Minneapolis: Klock and Klock, 1983.

Dickason, C. Fred. *Angels, Elect and Evil.* Chicago: Moody, 1975.

Douglas, J.D. ed. *Illustrated Bible Dictionary.* Wheaton: Tyndale, 1980.

Drawbridge, C. L. *Common Objections to Christianity.* London: R. S. Roxburghe House, 1914.

Dulles, Avery. *Models of Revelation.* Garden City, N. Y: Doubleday, 1983.

Elwell, Walter A., ed. *Evangelical Dictionary of Theology.* Grand Rapids: Baker, 1984.

Enns, Paul. *The Moody Handbook of Theology.* Chicago: Moody, 1989.

Erickson, Millard J. *Christian Theology.* Grand Rapids: Baker, 1983.

Erickson, Millard J., ed. *Readings in Christian Theology, Vol. 2.* Grand Rapids: Baker, 1976.

Evans, Robert F. *Pelagius– Inquires and Reappraisals.* New York: The Seabury Press, 1968.

Feinberg, Charles L. *Premillennialism or Amillennialism.* New York: American Board of Missions to the Jews, 1961.

Ferguson, Sinclair B., David F. Wright, J. I. Packer, eds. *New Dictionary of Theology.* Downers Grove, IL: InterVarsity, 1988.

Ferre, Nels R.S. *The Universal World.* Philadelphia: The Westminster Press, 1964.

Friesen, Harry. "A Critical Analysis of Universalism," Th.D. Dissertation, Dallas Theological Seminary, Dallas, Texas, 1968.

Fromow, George H. *Will the Church Pass Through the Tribulation?* London: Sovereign Grace Advent Testimony, n.d.

Geisler, Norman and Nix, William E. *A General Introduction to the Bible.* Chicago: Moody, 1986.

Geisler, Norman. *Christian Apologetics.* Grand Rapids: Baker, 1976.

Gerstner, John H. *Reasons for Faith.* Grand Rapids: Baker, 1967.

Gonzalez, Justo L. *Christian Thought.* Nashville: Abingdon, 1970.

Green, James Benjamin. *Studies in the Holy Spirit.* New York: Fleming H. Revell, 1936.

Griffith-Thomas, W.H. *How We Got Our Bible.* Dallas: Dallas Seminary Press, 1984.

Gundry, Robert H. *The Church and the Tribulation.* Grand Rapids: Zondervan, 1973.

Gundry, Stanley and Alan F. Johnson. *Tensions in Contemporary Theology.* Grand Rapids: Baker, 1976.

Hannah, John. "History of Church Doctrine 510," unpublished class notes, Summer, 1986.

Hill, William J. *The Three-Personed God.* Washington D.C., Catholic University Press, 1982.

Holloman, Henry W. Notes from Theology II, Professor at Talbot School of Theology. 1976.

Hodge, Charles. *Systematic Theology.* Vol. 2. Grand Rapids: Eerdmans, 1973.

Hoekema, Anthony A., *The Bible and the Future.* Grand Rapids: Eerdmans, 1979.

House, H. Wayne, "An Investigation of Black Liberation Theology," *Bibliotheca Sacra*, Vol. 139, 554 (April/June 1982):159-76.

House, H. Wayne, and Thomas Ice. *Dominion Theology: Blessing or Curse?* Portland, OR: Multnomah Press, 1988.

Howe, Frederick R. *Challenge and Response.* Grand Rapids: Zondervan, 1982.

Hoyt, Herman. *The End Times.* Chicago: Moody, 1969.

Joppie, A.S. *The Ministry of Angels.* Grand Rapids: Baker, 1953.

Jukes, Andrew. *The Names of God in Holy Scripture.* Grand Rapids: Kregel Publications, 1986.

Klaassen, Walter., ed. *Anabaptism in Outline.* Scottdale, PA: Herald Press, 1981.

Kligerman, Aaron J. *Messianic Prophecy in the O.T.* Grand Rapids: Zondervan, 1957.

Ladd, George Eldon. *The Blessed Hope.* Grand Rapids: Eerdmans, 1956.

Leith, John H. *Creeds of the Churches.* Richmond, VA: John Knox Press, rev. ed., 1973.

Lightner, Robert P. *The Death Christ Died.* Shaumberg, Ill.: Regular Baptist Press, 1983.

Long, Gary D. *Definite Atonement.* Philadelphia: Presbyterian and Reformed, 1977.

Ludwigson, R. *A Survey of Bible Prophecy.* Grand Rapids: Zondervan , 1973.

Luther, Martin. *The Book of Concord.* Philadelphia: Fortress Press, 1959.

MacPherson, Norman. *Triumph Through Tribulation.* Otego, N.Y.: First Baptist Church, 1944.

MacPherson, Dave. *The Incredible Cover-up.* Plainfield, N.J.: Logos International, 1975.

Mayhue, Richard. *Snatched Before the Storm! A Case for Pretribulation.* Winona Lake, IN: BMH Books, 1980.

McDowell, Josh. *Resurrection Factor.* San Bernadino: Here's Life, 1981.

McRae, William. *The Dynamics of Spiritual Gifts.* Grand Rapids: Zondervan, 1976.

Miley, John. *Systematic Theology.* Vol. 1. New York: Hunt and Eaton, 1892.

Moyer, Elgin. *Wycliffe Biographical Dictionary of The Church*. Chicago: Moody, 1982.

Mueller, John Theodore. *Christian Dogmatics*. St. Louis: Concordia, 1955.

Murray, John. *The Imputation of Adam's Sin*. Philipsburg, N.J.: Presbeterian and Reformed, 1959.

Nash, Ronald H. *The Concept of God*. Grand Rapids: Zondervan, 1983.

Needham, Mrs. George C. *Angels and Demons*. Chicago: Moody, n.d.

Ott, Ludwig. *Fundamentals of Catholic Dogma*. St. Louis: Herder Book Company, 1960.

Pache, René. *The Inspiration and Authority of Scripture*. Chicago: Moody, 1969.

Packer, James I. "The Way of Salvation," *Bibliotheca Sacra* Vol. 130, No. 517 (Jan/Mar.):3-11.

Palmer, Edwin H. *The Five Points of Calvinism*. Grand Rapids: Baker, 1972.

Payne, J. Barton. *The Imminent Appearing of Christ*. Grand Rapids: Eerdmans, 1962.

Pentecost, J. D. *Things to Come*. Findlay, Ohio: Dunham, 1959.

Picirilli, Robert E. "He Emptied Himself," *Biblical Viewpoint*, Vol. 3, No. 1 (April 1969):23-30.

Pinnock, Clark H. *Reason Enough*. Downer's Grove, Il.: InterVarsity, 1980.

Ramm, Bernard. *The God Who Makes a Difference*. Waco, TX.: Word Books, 1972.

Reese, Alexander. *The Approaching Advent of Christ*. London: Marshall, Morgan, Scott, 1932.

Reiter, Richard R., Feinberg, Paul D., Archer, Gleason L., and Moo, Douglas J. *The Rapture: Pre-, Mid-, Posttribulational?* Grand Rapids: Zondervan, 1984.

Rice, John R. *Our God Breathed Book-The Bible*. Murfreesboro, Tenn.: Sword of the Lord Publishers, 1969.

Rice, John R. *The Power of Pentecost or the Fullness of the Spirit*. Murfreesboro, Tenn.: Sword of the Lord Publishers, 1949.

Rose, George. *Tribulation Till Translation*. Glendale: Rose Publishing, 1942.

Ryrie, Charles C. *Dispensationalism Today*. Chicago: Moody, 1965.

_____. *Basic Theology*. Wheaton: Victor Books,1986.

_____. *Ryrie Study Bible*. Chicago: Moody, 1978.

_____. *The Holy Spirit*. Chicago: Moody, 1965.

Samarin, William J. *Tongues of Men and Angels*. New York: Macmillan, 1972.

Shannon, Franklin J. *John Wesley's Doctrine of Man*. Th. M. thesis, Dallas Theological Seminary: 1963.

Shedd, William G. T. *Dogmatic Theology*. Chicago: The Judson Press, 1907.

Soulen, Richard N. *Handbook of Biblical Criticism.* Atlanta: John Knox Press, 1976.

Spencer, Duane Edward. *TULIP.* Grand Rapids: Baker, 1979.

Sproul, R. C. *Reason to Believe.* Grand Rapids: Zondervan, 1982.

Steele, David N. and Curtis C. Thomas. *Five Points of Calvinism.* Philadelphia: Presbyterian and Reformed, 1965.

Stevens, W. Earle, "A Refutation of Universal Salvation" Th. M. thesis, Dallas Theological Seminary, 1942.

Strong, A. H. *Systematic Theology.* Westwood, N. J.: Revell, 1907.

Sumrall, Lester, *The Reality of Angels.* Nashville: Thomas Nelson, 1982.

Tan, Paul Lee. *The Interpretation of Prophecy:* Michigan: Cushing-Malloy, Inc., 1974.

Tenney, Merrill C. *The Zondervan Pictorial Encyclopedia of the Bible.* Grand Rapids: Zondervan, 1976.

The Greek New Testament. New York: American Bible Society, 1975.

Thiessen, Henry C. *Lectures in Systematic Theology.* Grand Rapids: Eerdmanns, 1979.

Thompson, F.C., ed. *The New Chain Reference Bible,* 4th ed., Indianapolis: B.B. Kirkbride Bible Co., Inc. 1964.

Toon, Peter and James Spiceland, eds. *One God In Trinity.* Westchester, Ill.: Cornerstone Books, 1982.

Toon, Peter. *Heaven and Hell.* Nashville: Thomas Nelson, 1986.

Torrey, R. A. *The Person and Work of the Holy Spirit.* New York: Fleming H. Revell, 1910.

Tozer, A. W. *The Knowledge of the Holy.* San Francisco: Harper & Row, 1961.

Unger, Merrill F. *Unger's Bible Dictionary.* Chicago: Moody, 1966.

Walker, Williston. *A History of the Christian Church.* New York: Scribners, 1970.

Walvoord, John F. *Jesus Christ Our Lord.* Chicago: Moody, 1969.

Walvoord, John F. and Roy B. Zuck, eds. *The Bible Knowledge Commentary, Vol. 2:New Testament* Wheaton: Victor Books, 1983.

_____. *The Millennial Kingdom.* Grand Rapids: Zondervan, 1959.

_____. *The Rapture Question.* Grand Rapids: Dunham Publishing, 1954.

_____. *The Blessed Hope and the Tribulation.* Grand Rapids: Zondervan, 1976.

Warfield, B.B. *The Plan of Salvation.* Grand Rapids: Eerdmans, 1935.

Witmer, John A. "The Inerrancy of the Bible;" *Walvoord: A Tribute.* Chicago: Moody, 1982.